WALL OF CONTROVERSY: CHURCH-STATE CONFLICT IN AMERICA

The Justices and their Opinions

Francis Graham Lee
Saint Joseph's University

ROBERT E. KRIEGER PUBLISHING COMPANY
MALABAR, FLORIDA
1986

Original Edition 1986

Printed and Published by
ROBERT E. KRIEGER PUBLISHING COMPANY, INC.
KRIEGER DRIVE
MALABAR, FL 32950

Copyright © 1986 by Robert E. Krieger Publishing Co., Inc.

All rights reserved. No part of this book may be reproduced in any form or by any electronic or mechanical means including information storage and retrieval systems without permission in writing from the publisher.
No liability is assumed with respect to the use of the information contained herein.

Printed in the United States of America

Library of Congress Cataloging-in-Publication Data

Lee, Francis Graham.
   Wall of controversy.

   1. Religious liberty—United States—Cases.
2. United States. Supreme Court. I. Title.
KF4783.A7L44   1986   342.73′0852   85-19697
ISBN 0-89874-828-3   347.302852

10 9 8 7 6 5 4 3 2

To my Daughters:
Elizabeth, Maureen, and Allison

That they may enjoy the freedom to follow in faith
in the well-trodden paths of the past.

Contents

Introduction: A Continuing Controversy 1
Chapter 1. The Historical Legacy 7
          Roger Williams, "The Ship Letter"
          James Madison, "Memorial and Remonstrance
          First Congress, "First Amendment Debate
          Section 1 of the Fourteenth Amendment
Chapter 2. Felix Frankfurter: The Secular Regulation Rule 18
          West Virginia State Board of Education v. Barnette (1943)
          Sherbert v. Verner (1963), John Marshall Harlan, dissenting opinion
Chapter 3. Hugo L. Black: Absolute Separationist 27
          Everson v. Board of Education (1947)
Chapter 4. William O. Douglas: Accommodationism 35
          Zorach v. Clauson (1952)
Chapter 5. Potter Stewart: No Coercion 41
          Abington Township v. Schempp (1963)
          Sherbert v. Verner (1963)
          Meek v. Pittenger (1975)
Chapter 6. William J. Brennan: The *Sherbert* and *Schempp* Tests 51
          Sherbert v. Verner (1963)
          Abington Township v. Schempp (1963)
          Walz v. Tax Commission (1970)
Chapter 7. Lewis F. Powell: The Three and One-Half Pronged Test 72
          Committee v. Nyquist (1973)
Chapter 8. Warren E. Burger: Balancing Free Exercise Claims 83
          Wisconsin v. Yoder (1972)
          United States v. Lee (1982)
          Bob Jones University v. United States (1983)
Chapter 9. William H. Rehnquist: A New Look at the Three-Pronged Test 100
          Mueller v. Allen (1983)
          Lynch v. Donnelly (1984), Warren E. Burger, opinion of the Court
Chapter 10. Conclusion: Beyond Neutrality: Toward a True Neutral Principle for the Religion Clauses 115
Index 121

INTRODUCTION

Alexis de Tocqueville, that most observant of all tourists to America, noted in his commentaries on American mores that there was hardly a dispute in America that did not eventually turn up in a court of law. De Tocqueville's observation, made early in the nineteenth century, is no less true now than then. Indeed, if anything, Americans are today a more litigious people, as reflected both in the Malthusian growth of lawyers and the equally exponential increase in the number of laws and regulations that govern our lives.

In fact, so accurate is de Tocqueville's observation that any student of American law becomes de facto a student of American history, of the American economic system, and of American society in general.

The steady rise in the number of criminal cases, of malpractice suits, and of divorce actions tells us as much as any volume of sociology about the changes that have overtaken America in the last two decades of the twentieth century. Though the dockets of our trial courts, both civil and criminal, are perhaps not as authoritative as the latest Gallup or Harris poll, they are probably as accurate an indicator of the problems of contemporary America as the agendas of our legislative bodies. Studied carefully, they reveal to us much about regional differences, about distinctions between urban, rural, and suburban life styles, and about the basic concerns of everyday Americans.

The docket of the United States Supreme Court reflects this diversity as well, underscoring what seems to be at any given time the most crucial national issues, telling us of the nation's values, its problems, and its hopes.

The Court's docket also tells us in part how well the system is functioning, how well it is addressing itself to the problems of American politics, and to what degree it is solving these problems so as to remove them from the political agenda. This latter capability is not a bad barometer of a political system's performance, as the political scientist Herbert Spiro has astutely pointed out in his work, particularly in his book *Government by Constitution*. According to Spiro, the success of a political system can be very effectively measured by its results, more specifically, by its ability to solve its problems—those factors identified as preventing the system from achieving its commonly held goals.

The fact, for instance, that the Soviet political and economic systems today seem as far as ever from solving the crisis of Soviet agriculture says something about the effectiveness of those systems. That the French political system up until the Fifth Republic was still frequently embroiled with questions about the very nature of the system's basic rules; that Canada, after over a hundred years as a state, still finds its politics torn by disputes over the question of whether it is one or two nations—these are accurate and reliable indicators of the weaknesses or failings, past or present, of the governments of these countries.

True, political systems will always witness conflict. Societies will always be plagued with problems. A system, however, that faces the same conflict over a long period of time or a society plagued with one problem for several decades is not functioning effectively. While it might survive for a long time, it will just as probably fall eventually or be radically changed if it never succeeds in resolving or removing from public debate such a long-standing, long-enduring problem.

In America, the Supreme Court, although supposedly one of three equal branches of government, has recently played a major, perhaps dominant, role in the business of resolving—if not always solving—domestic problems. In fact, the growth of the Court's importance since the early fifties can be explained largely in terms of its effectiveness in tackling societal problems that the other branches of government have been either unable or unwilling to handle.

The example of segregation comes immediately to mind. In 1954 neither the President nor Congress was ready to handle this problem, let alone solve it. Only the Court was willing to take hold of this political hot potato. The fact that today hardly anyone defends segregation is a tribute to the Court's success in handling what Gunnar Myrdal so aptly titled *The American Dilemma*. Sex discrimination is a more contemporary issue in which the Court has taken the lead—a lead which Congress, the President, and, most importantly, the American people have followed.

Examining the caseload of the Court turns up other examples of problems that have worked their way up to the Court in the form of cases—problems that have gradually vanished, frequently because the Court has "solved" them. Hardly a year passed in the fifties, for instance, in which the Court was not faced with a case that pitted the interests of internal security against the liberty of the First Amendment. That issue today is essentially dead. The Court's decisions have effectively ended it as a controversy in American political life. Similarly, close Court watchers would know that obscenity, the "tar baby" of the Court since *Roth v. California* (1957), no longer makes an annual appearance before the Justices. They must now pay, like the rest of the citizenry, to see XXX-rated movies. Instead of internal security and obscenity cases, we now have cases generated by the issues of abortion and affirmative action. These issues also will probably disappear from the judicial landscape in the next decade, as the struggles with segregation and obscenity have apparently already passed onto the pages of judicial history.

One issue, however, has refused to go away: this is the conflict of church and state. Free exercise controversies have troubled the modern Court since 1940 and, although the religious groups involved and the specific controversies have changed, the overriding issue has remained the same. The establishment imbroglio has witnessed even less change: aid to religious schools and prayers in public schools are still very much the nub of the dispute. Even the lawyers have remained much the same group: Leo Pfeffer and William Ball have litigated the lion's share of these cases and can probably bank on a good number of similar cases in the future if they are so inclined.

What explains this phenomenon—this failure? Why has the Court succeeded in rooting out de jure segregation, in establishing a modus vivendi regarding obscenity, and even in enunciating a position on political speech that seems acceptable to both liberals and conservatives—yet failed totally in settling the controversy involving the relationship between religion and the state?

One possible explanation is that the Court's reasoning on this subject has not persuaded the parties involved that the Court is right and that they should give up the battle. As Alexander Hamilton so wisely pointed out, the Court, possessed of neither the purse nor the sword, has only the power to persuade—and when this fails, *it* fails.

But why has it failed to persuade on this issue despite much effort? The language of the Constitution seems clear enough:

Congress shall make no law respecting an establishment of religion, or prohibiting the free exercise thereof.

The basic issue that the religion clauses—or are they participial phrases?—pose for the Court is also relatively clear. As Professor Dallin Oaks (later a Justice of the Utah Supreme Court and now an Elder of the Mormon Church), has pointed out: the establishment clause essentially asks how much cooperation can exist between government and religion without constituting the forbidden establishment; the free exercise clause asks how much nonconformity must be tolerated in the name of religious liberty.

The dilemma arises, therefore, not from the Constitution but rather from the interpretation the Court has given to the Constitution—the manner in which it has sought to answer Oaks's deceptively simple questions. The Justices have been less than clear on many accounts and, perhaps because of this, less than convincing. Certainly, this has not been due to lack of effort. A minidictionary of terms has been created: the establishment clause alone has added to the language of the law such concepts as: wall of separation, child-benefit, permissible accommodation, and excessive entanglement, to mention but a few. The free exercise dispute has witnessed the Court executing an almost 180 degree shift from *Reynolds v. United States*–1878 (reaffirmed as recently as 1961 in *Braunfeld v. Brown*) to *Sherbert v. Verner* (1963) and *Wisconsin v. Yoder* (1972). With these latter cases, it rejected what Bowdoin College's Richard Morgan has labelled "the secular regulation rule" and replaced it with the Court's current efforts at balancing the interests of the individual and those of society.

The problem thus cannot be attributed to any want of trying. The Court has labored long and hard, though many dispute whether it has labored well. It has, as evidenced by the free exercise cases, been willing to strike out along new paths, abandoning both the habits and precedents of its past. On the establishment front, it slowly assembled the three-pronged test: "secular purpose" deriving from *Everson v. Board of Education* (1947), "purpose and primary effect" taken from *McGowan V. Marvland* (1961), and, from *Walz v. Tax Commission* (1971), "no excessive entanglement." First employed by Chief Justice Warren Burger in *Lemon v. Kurtzman* (1971), the three-pronged test remains, at least officially, the Court's standard for establishment clause cases.

Throughout this process, the Court has consistently posited the value of neutrality as representing the proper, i.e., constitutional, relationship between church and state. The requirements of "secular purpose," "primary effect," "no excessive entanglement," and minimum "divisiveness" all seem to represent attempts to operationalize the concept of neutrality. In practice, they may remind one of the Supreme Court's efforts not too long ago to give meaning to the concept of obscenity as constitutionally unprotected speech, an effort that caused a whole host of frequently confusing terms, e.g., "patently offensive," "utterly without redeeming social importance," and "pandering," to be entered into the legal lexicon. Justice Potter Stewart was probably the most forthright on this score when he acknowledged in *Jacobellis v. Ohio* (1964): ". . . I could never succeed in intelligently [defining it]. . . . But I know it when I see it and . . . [this] is not that."

Stewart's remark is wonderful comedy for a constitutional law course, but probably it got few guffaws from members of police vice squads serious about enforcing antismut ordinances and fewer still from prosecutors charged with getting convictions under such statutes.

In fact, Stewart's admission was a frank and honest confession of failure and probably foretold Stewart's eventual conversion to the Black-Douglas position on obscenity. Had this switch occurred prior to Black's retirement, it would have meant that all antiobscenity statutes would be struck down as being in violation of the First Amendment. Yet, despite the Court's less than stellar performance vis-à-vis obscenity, it should be noted that the decisions themselves, specifically their results, pointed rather consistently in one direction: greater freedom to publish and to read whatever one wanted, free from the threat of government prosecution.

This has not been true concerning the Court's decisions on religion, particularly those dealing with the establishment clause. Both the tests and the results have been confusing. "Primary effect," for example, has clearly been interpreted in two different ways. Chief Justice Burger and Associate Justice White seem to emphasize the notion of first effect. (See White's opinion of the Court in *Board of Education v. Allen* (1968) and Burger for the Court in *Lemon v. Kurtzman* (1971).) In contrast, Justice Powell, in *Committee v. Nyquist* (1973), seems to read it as meaning the overall effect. "Excessive entanglement" and "divisivensss" have fared no better while "secular purpose" has proved broad enough to drive a school bus through—and school prayers as well.

The Court's quandary on the establishment issue was probably clearest in the 1977 case of *Wolman v. Walter*. The Court, ruling on a multifaceted Ohio program of aid to nonpublic schools, produced no less than five different configurations of Justices in the process of upholding diagnostic testing for educational handicaps (8–1), therapeutic services for educationally-handicapped students (7–2), and textbooks, standardized tests and scoring (6–3)—while invalidating field trips (5–4) and instructional materials (6–3). In comparison to the Burger Court's performance in *Wolman*, the Warren Court's record on obscenity is a model of unanimity and cogent thinking.

Free exercise cases under the Burger Court have been only a little less confused. After appearing to follow the Warren Court's *Sherbert* (1963) decision in *Wisconsin v. Yoder* (1972), with the result that the free exercise clause was read as allowing an "incidental burden on the free exercise of . . . religion [only if] . . . justified by a 'compelling state interest in the regulation of a subject within the State's constitutional power to regulate. . . .'"—though the Chief Justice admittedly seemed more comfortable with the concept of "balancing" than with the standard of "compelling state interest"—the Burger Court's more recent decisions seem to be tipping the scales in favor of government. The claim of Edwin Lee (*U.S. v. Lee*–1982), a member of the Old Order Amish, seems only slightly less serious than that of Yoder. Indeed, Lee's request for an exemption from social security coverage was accepted by the Court as sincerely made, but it was, according to a unanimous Court, outweighed by the government's interest in including as many people as possible in the social security program. How this interest is greater than that of the state of Wisconsin in universal education (*Yoder*) is not made abundantly clear.

Equally troubling on the free exercise front was the Court's subsequent decision in the case of *Bob Jones University* (1983). Again the free exercise claim was adjudged sincere; it fell, however, before what Chief Justice Burger characterized as the need to deny the benefit of tax-exempt status to organizations involved in an "activity . . . contrary to a fundamental public policy [i.e., the end of segregation]." This fact, wrote Burger, is enough to demonstrate that "the governmental interest at stake is compelling" and hence, superior to any religious liberty claim. If that is the case, the nineteenth century actions by the federal government in threatening to seize Mormon Church property because of the Mormon support of polygamy would still be constitutional, and the tax-exempt status of all-male Catholic seminaries would be open to question, given society's current commitment to ending sex discrimination.

Cooler heads will say that this argument is extreme: the Burger Court is not likely to strip Roman Catholic seminaries of their exempt status because of the Church's refusal to ordain women. The same voices of sweet reasonableness would also say that Edwin Lee lost because the Court was concerned that by granting his claim it would soon find itself faced with a more ticklish issue—whether religious pacifists could claim exemption from that portion of their federal income taxes that goes to the military.

In fact, the voices of reason and common sense would defend the Court's actions regarding both free exercise and establishment as being realistic, politically sound, and, at bottom, pragmatic. They may be all three, but a Court that is solely realistic, political, and pragmatic may have problems convincing the realistic, pragmatic, and political types that inhabit the halls of the Congress and the White House that it is the Constitution, and not the Justices, speaking. They may fail—in fact, in the realm of religion they *have* failed to persuade. Consequently, they find their decisions in this arena scorned by a majority of Americans and, not surprisingly, transformed into political issues. Such surely is the case with prayers in public schools and possibly with the issue of aid to religious schools. These problems, rather than being resolved, seem to have been aggravated and even inflamed as a result of the Court's ministering.

The purpose of this book is to encourage further exploration and discussion of the issues that arise out of the Constitution's guarantees of religious freedom, which are likely to be on society's political agenda for several more decades. First, it will present to the reader excerpts from a few of the documents that may shed light on the meaning and effect of the First Amendment guarantees; second, and most important, it will discuss the major religious liberty cases and the Justices who have played the most significant role in the last half century in interpreting this section of the Constitution; finally, it will briefly examine what the Burger Court has sought to accomplish in the past several years and look into the future to suggest a way out of the present morass.

Chapter 1 THE HISTORICAL LEGACY

Appeals to "the intent of the framers" are frequently made in constitutional disputes. Efforts to determine *wie es eigenlich qewesen*, to use von Ranke's phrase, have occupied the energies of many constitutional historians, and yet, despite the major forays that have been made in the past and doubtless will continue in the future, the answer probably never can be ascertained with anything approaching true certainty. The dispassionate observer must conclude with Chief Justice Warren, who found in *Brown v. Board of Education* (1954)—having sifted through the historical controversies surrounding the adoption of the equal protection clause—". . . that, although these sources cast some light, it is not enough to resolve the problem with which we are faced."

Still, while history may not be able to provide a final response, it surely provides a starting point that should not be ignored. The ideas of Thomas Jefferson and James Madison or those of Roger Williams are not to be cast aside simply because they do not furnish us with a definitive answer as to whether silent meditation or tuition tax credits are or are not constitutional. Likewise, the debates in Congress—limited as such records are —should not be overlooked by anyone seriously concerned with looking beyond the immediate questions of whether public school prayer or diagnostic testing for children in parochial schools is permissible.

Jefferson, Madison, and Williams all played major roles in developing the American attitudes about church-state relations that led to the adoption of the First Amendment in 1791. Each can claim the title "champion of religious liberty," but the motives that directed them were quite different. Williams believed in religious liberty because he feared that government would seek to use religion, and thereby corrupt it, for government's purposes. Jefferson and Madison dreaded the opposite: that religion would control government. By embracing the Jeffersonian-Madisonian view in *Everson v. Board of Education*–1947 (See Black: "Absolute Separationist") the Court elected to follow a path quite different from the one they would have gone down had they seen in Roger Williams the primary American progenitor of religious freedom.

The Congressional debates on the First Amendment provide another key element that needs to be examined in order better to understand the meaning and purpose of the religion clauses. James Madison obviously was the major force in the House of Representatives during the First Congress. However, just as Jefferson has been allowed, perhaps unfairly, to overshadow Williams, so Madison's work has all but blotted out the contributions of other members of Congress. Most notable is Samuel Livermore of New Hampshire, who, as Canon Anson Phelps Stokes has noted, played a significant role in the development of the thinking in Congress on religious liberty.

Finally, there is the Fourteenth Amendment, more particularly the first section of the Fourteenth Amendment—in which the due process clause carries over, absorbs, or incorporates those rights that are "implicit in the concept of ordered liberty" (opinion of the Court by Justice Cardozo in *Palko v. Connecticut*–1937) or "fundamental to the American scheme of justice" (Justice Byron White for the Court in *Duncan v. Louisiana*–1968).

Aside from the apparently dead issue of whether the Fourteenth Amendment was intended to make the Bill of Rights binding on the states, there is the much-forgotten question of whether nonestablishment is a "liberty" or one of "the privileges or immunities" in the same sense as free speech, free press, or free exercise of religion—and thus open to be incorporated via the first section of the Fourteenth Amendment. Perhaps more serious consideration, rather than the ex post facto justifications that have been presented in the past, would better serve in the solution of the vexatious problems the Court has faced in grappling with the establishment clause.

Though ignored by the Justices in their opinions in *Everson* (1947), Roger Williams was surely the earliest American exponent of religious liberty. Driven from the Massachusetts Bay Colony by the intolerant Puritan divines, Williams settled in Rhode Island. Considered the founder of American Baptists, he presents a defense of religious liberty that posits the dangers that overclose church-state cooperation poses for the church. Two of his writings on this subject are particularly important: *Bloudy Tenent*, described by the eminent church historian Canon Stokes as "an enlargement of Williams' view that 'God requireth not an uniformity of Religion;'" and the "Ship Letter" written by Williams during the end of 1654 and beginning of 1655, after he had been chosen to lead the Providence settlement. It is as follows:

> There goes many a ship to sea, with many hundred souls in one ship, whose weal and woe is common, and is a true picture of a commonwealth, or a human combination or society. It hath fallen out sometimes, that both papists and protestants, Jews and Turks, may be embarked in one ship; upon which supposal I affirm, that all the liberty of conscience, that ever I pleaded for, turns upon these two hinges—that none of the papists, protestants, Jews, or Turks, be forced to come to the ship's prayers or worship, nor compelled from their own particular prayers or worship, if they practice any. I further add, that I never denied, that notwithstanding this liberty, the commander of this ship ought to command the ship's course, yea, and also command that justice, peace and sobriety, be kept and practiced, both among the seamen and all the passengers. If any of the seamen refuse to perform their services, or passengers to pay their freight; if any refuse to help, in person or purse, towards the common charges or defence; if any refuse to obey the common laws and orders of the ship, concerning their common peace of preservation; if any shall mutiny and rise up against their commanders and officers; if any should preach or write that there ought to be no commanders or officers, because all are equal in Christ, therefore no masters nor officers, no laws nor orders, nor corrections nor punishments;—I say, I never denied, but in such cases, whatever is pretended, the commander or commanders may judge, resist, compel and punish such transgressors, according to their deserts and merits.

The legacy of Madison and Jefferson is so extensive that no short summary treatment such as this book is able to give can do it justice. Chief among Jefferson's contributions is his "Bill for Establishing Religious Freedom." First proposed in 1779 and finally adopted in 1785, it began the process of disestablishing the Episcopal church in Virginia. Even more important, and containing most of Jefferson's ideas, is Madison's "Memorial and Remonstrance." The "Memorial" was written by Madison to head off efforts by Patrick Henry and others to provide state funding for religious instruction.

MEMORIAL AND REMONSTRANCE AGAINST RELIGIOUS ASSESSMENTS

To The Honorable the General Assembly
of
The Commonwealth of Virginia.
A Memorial and Remonstrance.

We, the subscribers, citizens of the said Commonwealth, having taken into serious consideration, a Bill printed by order of the last Session of General

Assembly, entitled "A Bill establishing a provision for Teachers of the Christian Religion," and conceiving that the same, if finally armed with the sanctions of a law, will be a dangerous abuse of power, are bound as faithful members of a free State, to remonstrate against it, and to declare the reasons by which we are determined. We remonstrate against the said Bill,

1. Because we hold it for a fundamental and undeniable truth, "that Religion or the duty which we owe to our Creator and the Manner of discharging it, can be directed only by reason and conviction, not by force or violence." The Religion then of every man must be left to the conviction and conscience of every man; and it is the right of every man to exercise it as these may dictate. This right is in its nature an unalienable right. It is unalienable; because the opinions of men, depending only on the evidence contemplated by their own minds, cannot follow the dictates of other men: It is unalienable also; because what is here a right towards men, is a duty towards the Creator. It is the duty of every man to render to the Creator such homage, and such only, as he believes to be acceptable to him. This duty is precedent both in order of time and degree of obligation, to the claims of Civil Society. Before any man can be considered as a member of Civil Society, he must be considered as a subject of the Governor of the Universe: And if a member of Civil Society, who enters into any subordinate Association, must always do it with a reservation of his duty to the general authority; much more must every man who becomes a member of any particular Civil Society, do it with a saving of his allegiance to the Universal Sovereign. We maintain therefore that in matters of Religion, no man's right is abridged by the institution of Civil Society, and that Religion is wholly exempt from its cognizance. True it is, that no other rule exists, by which any question which may divide a Society, can be ultimately determined, but the will of the majority; but it is also true, that the majority may trespass on the rights of the minority.

2. Because if religion be exempt from the authority of the Society at large, still less can it be subject to that of the Legislative Body. The latter are but the creatures and vicegerents of the former. Their jurisdiction is both derivative and limited: it is limited with regard to the coordinate departments, more necessarily is it limited with regard to the constituents. The preservation of a free government requires not merely, that the metes and bounds which separate each department of power may be invariably maintained; but more especially, that neither of them be suffered to overleap the great Barrier which defends the rights of the people. The Rulers who are guilty of such an encroachment, exceed the commission from which they derive their authority, and are Tyrants. The People who submit to it are governed by laws made neither by themselves, nor by an authority derived from them, and are slaves.

3. Because, it is proper to take alarm at the first experiment on our liberties. We hold this prudent jealousy to be the first duty of citizens, and one of [the] noblest characteristics of the late Revolution. The freemen of America did not wait till usurped power had strengthened itself by exercise, and entangled the question in

precedents. They saw all the consequences in the principle, and they avoided the consequences by denying the principle. We revere this lesson too much, soon to forget it. Who does not see that the same authority which can establish Christianity, in exclusion of all other Religions, may establish with the same ease any particular sect of Christians, in exclusion of all other Sects? That the same authority which can force a citizen to contribute three pence only of his property for the support of any one establishment, may force him to conform to any other establishment in all cases whatsoever?

4. Because, the bill violates that equality which ought to be the basis of every law, and which is more indispensible, in proportion as the validity or expediency of any law is more liable to be impeached. If "all men are by nature equally free and independent," all men are to be considered as entering into Society on equal conditions; as relinquishing no more, and therefore retaining no less, one than another, of their natural rights. Above all are they to be considered as retaining an "*equal* title to the free exercise of Religion according to the dictates of conscience" Whilst we assert for ourselves a freedom to embrace, to profess and to observe the Religion which we believe to be of divine origin, we cannot deny an equal freedom to those whose minds have not yet yielded to the evidence which has convinced us. If this freedom be abused, it is an offence against God, not against man: To God, therefore, not to men, must an account of it be rendered. As the Bill violates equality by subjecting some to peculiar burdens; so it violates the same principle, by granting to others peculiar exemptions. Are the Quakers and Menonists the only sects who think a compulsive support of their religions unnecessary and unwarantable? Can their piety alone be intrusted with the care of public worship? Ought their Religions to be endowed above all others, with extraordinary privileges, by which proselytes may be enticed from all others? We think too favorably of the justice and good sense of these denominations, to believe that they either covet preeminencies over their fellow citizens, or that they will be seduced by them, from the common opposition to the measure.

5. Because the bill implies either that the Civil Magistrate is a competent Judge of Religious truth; or that he may employ Religion as an engine of Civil policy. The first is an arrogant pretension falsified by the contradictory opinions of Rulers in all ages, and throughout the world: The second an unhallowed perversion of the means of salvation.

6. Because the establishment proposed by the Bill is not requisite for the support of the Christian Religion. To say that it is, is a contradiction to the Christian Religion itself; for every page of it disavows a dependence on the powers of this world: it is a contradiction to fact; for it is known that this Religion both existed and flourished, not only without the support of human laws, but in spite of every opposition from them; and not only during the period of miraculous aid, but long after it had been left to its own evidence, and the ordinary care of Providence: Nay, it is a contradiction in terms; for a Religion not invented by human policy, must

have preexisted and been supported, before it was established by human policy. It is moreover to weaken in those who profess this Religion a pious confidence in its innate excellence, and the patronage of its Author; and to foster in those who still reject it, a suspicion that its friends are too conscious of its fallacies, to trust it to its own merits.

7. Because experience witnesseth that ecclesiastical establishments, instead of maintaining the purity and efficacy of Religion, have had a contrary operation. During almost fifteen centuries has the legal establishment of Christianity been on trial. What have been its fruits? More or less in all places, pride and indolence in the Clergy; ignorance and servility in the laity; in both, superstition, bigotry and persecution. Enquire of the Teachers of Christianity for the ages in which it appeared in its greatest lustre; those of every sect point to the ages prior to its incorporation with Civil policy. Propose a restoration of this primitive state in which its Teachers depended on the voluntary rewards of their flocks; many of them predict its downfall. On which side ought their testimony to have greatest weight, when for or when against their interest?

8. Because the establishment in question is not necessary for the support of Civil Government. If it be urged as necessary for the support of Civil Government only as it is a means of supporting Religion, and it be not necessary for the latter purpose, it cannot be necessary for the former. If Religion be not within [the] cognizance of Civil Government, how can its legal establishment be said to be necessary to civil Government? What influence in fact have ecclesiastical establishments had on Civil Society? In some instances they have been seen to erect a spiritual tyranny on the ruins of Civil authority; in many instances they have been seen upholding the thrones of political tyranny; in no instance have they been seen the guardians of the liberties of the people. Rulers who wished to subvert the public liberty, may have found an established clergy convenient auxiliaries. A just government, instituted to secure & perpetuate it, needs them not. Such a government will be best supported by protecting every citizen in the enjoyment of his Religion with the same equal hand which protects his person and his property; by neither invading the equal rights of any Sect, nor suffering any Sect to invade those of another.

9. Because the proposed establishment is a departure from that generous policy, which, offering an asylum to the persecuted and oppressed of every Nation and Religion, promised a lustre to our country, and an accession to the number of its citizens. What a melancholy mark is the Bill of sudden degeneracy? Instead of holding forth an asylum to the persecuted, it is itself a signal of persecution. It degrades from the equal rank of Citizens all those whose opinions in Religion do not bend to those of the Legislative authority. Distant as it may be, in its present form, from the Inquisition it differs from it only in degree. The one is the first step, the other the last in the career of intolerance. The magnanimous sufferer under this cruel scourge in foreign Regions must view the Bill as a Beacon on our Coast,

warning him to seek some other haven, where liberty and philanthropy in their due extent may offer a more certain repose from his troubles.

10. Because, it will have a like tendency to banish our Citizens. The allurements presented by other situations are every day thinning their number. To superadd a fresh motive to emigration, by revoking the liberty which they now enjoy, would be the same species of folly which has dishonoured and depopulated flourishing kingdoms.

11. Because, it will destroy that moderation and harmony which the forbearance of our laws to intermeddle with Religion, has produced amongst its several sects. Torrents of blood have been spilt in the old world, by vain attempts of the secular arm to extinguish Religious discord, by proscribing all difference in Religious opinions. Time has at length revealed the true remedy. Every relaxation of narrow and rigorous policy, wherever it has been tried, has been found to assuage the disease. The American Theatre has exhibited proofs; that equal and compleat liberty, if it does not wholly eradicate it, sufficiently destroys its malignant influence on the health and prosperity of the State. If with the salutary effects of this system under our own eyes, we begin to contract the bonds of Religious freedom, we know no name that will too severely reproach our folly. At least let warning be taken at the first fruits of the threatened innovation. The very appearance of the Bill has transformed that "Christian forbearance, love and charity," which of late mutually prevailed, into animosities and jealousies, which may not soon be appeased. What mischiefs may not be dreaded should this enemy to the public quiet be armed with the force of a law?

12. Because, the policy of the bill is adverse to the diffusion of the light of Christianity. The first wish of those who enjoy this precious gift, ought to be that it may be imparted to the whole race of mankind. Compare the number of those who have as yet received it with the number still remaining under the dominion of false Religions; and how small is the former! Does the policy of the Bill tend to lessen the disproportion? No; it at once discourages those who are strangers to the light of [revelation] from coming into the Region of it; and countenances, by example the nations who continue in darkness, in shutting out those who might convey it to them. Instead of levelling as far as possible, every obstacle to the victorious progress of truth, the Bill with an ignoble and unchristian timidity would circumscribe it, with a wall of defence, against the encroachments of error.

13. Because attempts to enforce by legal sanctions, acts obnoxious to so great a proportion of Citizens, tend to enervate the laws in general, and to slacken the bands of Society. If it be difficult to execute any law which is not generally deemed necessary or salutary, what must be the case where it is deemed invalid and dangerous? and what may be the effect of so striking an example of impotency in the Government, on its general authority.

14. Because a measure of such singular magnitude and delicacy ought not to be

imposed, without the clearest evidence that it is called for by a majority of citizens: and no satisfactory method is yet proposed by which the voice of the majority in this case may be determined, or its influence secured. "The people of the respective counties are indeed requested to signify their opinion respecting the adoption of the Bill to the next Session of Assembly." But the representation must be made equal, before the voice either of the Representatives or of the Counties, will be that of the people. Our hope is that neither of the former will, after due consideration, espouse the dangerous principle of the Bill. Should the event disappoint us, it will still leave us in full confidence, that a fair appeal to the latter will reverse the sentence against our liberties.

15. Because, finally, "the equal right of every citizen to the free exercise of his Religion according to the dictates of conscience" is held by the same tenure with all our other rights. If we recur to its origin, it is equally the gift of nature; if we weigh its importance, it cannot be less dear to us; if we consult the Declaration of those rights which pertain to the good people of Virginia, as the "basis and foundation of Government," it is enumerated with equal solemnity, or rather studied emphasis. Either then, we must say, that the will of the Legislature is the only measure of their authority; and that in the plentitude of this authority, they may sweep away all our fundamental rights; or, that they are bound to leave this particular right untouched and sacred: Either we must say, that they may controul the freedom of the press, may abolish the trial by jury, may swallow up the Executive and Judiciary Powers of the State; nay that they may despoil us of our very right of suffrage, and erect themselves into an independent and hereditary assembly: or we must say, that they have no authority to enact into law the Bill under consideration. We the subscribers say, that the General Assembly of this Commonwealth have no such authority: And that no effort may be omitted on our part against so dangerous an usurpation, we oppose to it, this remonstrance; earnestly praying, as we are in duty bound, that the Supreme Lawgiver of the Universe, by illuminating those to whom it is addressed, may on the one hand, turn their councils from every act which would affront his holy prerogative, or violate the trust committed to them: and on the other, guide them into every measure which may be worthy of his [blessing, may re]dound to their own praise, and may establish more firmly the liberties, the prosperity, and the Happiness of the Commonwealth.

II Madison, 183–191

The establishment and free exercise clauses are products of the First Congress. Under the leadership of James Madison of Virginia, the House of Representatives took the initiative to respond to the demand of those who had found the absence of such guarantees to be a defect in the Constitution. The most substantive part of the debate on the religion clauses took place in the House on August 15, 1789, and is reprinted below.

Saturday, August 15,
AMENDMENTS TO THE CONSTITUTION

The House again went into a Committee of the Whole on the proposed amendments to the Constitution. Mr. Boudinot in the Chair.

The fourth proposition being under consideration as follows:

Article 1. Section 9. Between paragraphs two and three insert "no religion shall be established by law nor Shall the equal rights of concience be infringed."

MR. SYLVESTER had some doubts of the propriety of the mode of expression used in this paragraph. He apprehended that it was liable to a construction different from what had been made by the committee. He feared it might be thought to have a tendency to abolish religion altogether.

MR. VINING suggested the propriety of transposing the two members of the sentence.

MR. GERRY said it would read better if it was, that no religious doctrine shall be established by law.

MR. SHERMAN thought the amendment altogether unnecessary, inasmuch as Congress had no authority whatever delegated to them by the Constitution to make religious establishments; he would, therefore, move to have it struck out.

MR. CARROLL—As the rights of conscience are, in their nature, of peculiar delicacy, and will little bear the gentlest touch of governmental hand; and as many sects have concurred in opinion that they are not well secured under the present Constitution, he said he was much in favor of adopting the words. He thought it would tend more towards conciliating the minds of the people to the Government than almost any other amendment he had heard proposed. He would not contend with gentlemen about the phraseology, his object was to secure the substance in such a manner as to satisfy the wishes of the honest part of the community.

MR. MADISON said, he apprehended the meaning of the words to be, that Congress should not establish a religion, and enforce the legal observation of it by law, nor compel men to worship God in any manner contrary to their conscience. Whether the words are necessary or not, he did not mean to say, but they had been required by some of the State Conventions, who seemed to entertain an opinion that under the clause of the Constitution which gave power to Congress to make all laws necessary and proper to carry into execution the Constitution, and the laws made under it, enabled them to make laws of such a nature as might infringe the rights of conscience, and establish a national religion; to prevent these effects he presumed the amendment was intended, and he thought it as well expressed as the nature of the language would admit.

MR. HUNTINGTON said that he feared, with the gentleman first up on this subject, that the words might be taken in such latitude as to be extremely hurtful to the cause of religion. He understood the amendment to mean what had been expressed by the gentleman from Virginia; but others might find it convenient to put another construction upon it. The ministers of the congregations to the Eastward were maintained by the contributions of those who belonged to their society; the expense of building meeting-houses was contributed in the same manner. These things were regulated by by-laws. If an action was brought before a Federal Court on any of these cases, the person who had neglected to perform his engagements could not be compelled to do it; for a support of ministers or building of places of worship might be construed into a religious establishment.

By the charter of Rhode Island, no religion could be established by law: he could give a history of the effects of such a regulation; indeed the people were now enjoying the blessed fruits of it. He hoped, therefore, the amendment would be made in such a way as to secure the rights of conscience, and a free exercise of the rights of religion, but not to patronise those who professed no religion at all.

MR. MADISON thought if the word "national" was inserted before religion, it would satisfy the minds of honorable gentlemen. He believed that the people feared one sect might obtain a pre-eminence, or two combine together, and establish a religion to which they would compel others to conform. He thought if the word "national" was introduced, it would point the amendment directly to the object it was intended to prevent.

MR. LIVERMORE was not satisfied with that amendment; but he did not wish them to dwell long on the subject. He thought it would be better if it were altered and made to read in this manner, that Congress shall make no laws touching religion or infringing the rights of conscience.

MR. GERRY did not like the term national, proposed by the gentleman from Virginia, and he hoped it would not be adopted by the House. It brought to his mind some observations that had taken place in the conventions at the time they were considering the present Constitution. It had been insisted upon by those who were called anit-federalists that this form of Government consolidated the Union; the honorable gentleman's motion shows that he considers it in the same light. Those who were called anti-federalists at that time, complained that they had injustice done them by the title, because they were in favor of a Federal Government and the others were in favor of a national one; the federalists were for ratifying the Constitution as it stood and the others not until amendments were made. Their names then ought not to have been distinguished by federalist and anit-federalists, but rats and anti-rats.

MR. MADISON withdrew his motion, but observed that the words "no national religion shall be established by law," did not imply that the Government was a national one; the question was then taken on MR. LIVERMORE'S motion and passed in the affirmative, thirty-one for and twenty against it.

Next to the Bill of Rights itself, the Fourteenth Amendment is the most important statement of individual rights found in the American Constitution. Proposed by Congress in 1866, it was ratified by the requisite number of states in 1868. A product of changes wrought by the Civil War, the Amendment was born in controversy and has produced more than its share of strife in the years since. Indeed, it is now the most litigated part of the Constitution. Precisely what the principal framers, Congressman John Bingham of Ohio and Senator Jacob Howard of Michigan, intended will probably never be known, much less what the members of Congress intended when they voted to propose it to the states. The root of most of the ensuing controversy is section 1, the section that incorporates the free exercise and establishment clauses.

Article XIV

Section 1. All persons born or naturalized in the United States, and subject to the jurisdiction thereof, are citizens of the United States and of the State wherein they reside. No State shall make or enforce any law which shall abridge the privileges or immunities of citizens of the United States; nor shall any State deprive any person of life, liberty, or property, without due process of law; nor deny to any person within its jurisdiction the equal protection of the laws.

Chapter 2 FELIX FRANKFURTER: THE SECULAR REGULATION RULE

When pressed to be more precise as to what he meant by the sobriquet "strict constructionist," President Richard Nixon replied that his desire was to staff the Supreme Court with Justices cast in the likeness of Felix Frankfurter. During his twenty-three-year career on the High Court, Felix Frankfurter—Harvard law professor, social reformer, and Roosevelt brain truster—had established himself as mid-twentieth century America's leading spokesman for the philosophy of judicial self-restraint, enthusiastically assuming the mantle of Oliver Wendell Holmes, Jr. and James Bradley Thayer. Indeed, in the minds of many, Frankfurter had succeeded not only in following in the footsteps of Holmes and Thayer, but also in going further than his masters in establishing barriers against what he saw as dangerous intrusions by the judiciary into the process of democratic decision making.

Like the little Dutch boy with his finger in the dike, Frankfurter sought throughout his judicial career to restrain the activist impulses of his brethren, constantly reminding them that, as "the least democratic branch" and least powerful unit of government, they should beware of imposing their opinions—

whether couched in the language of the Constitution or not—on Congress and the President.

Believing that self-restraint is too rare a virtue among the types that frequently come to the Court—many fresh from the battles of the political arena—Frankfurter made himself the acknowledged expert in using what the University of Virginia's Henry J. Abraham has referred to as the "maxims of judicial self-restraint." The doctrines of "case or controversy," standing, ripeness, and mootness were skillfully employed and, indeed, refined in Frankfurter's hands. This served to steer his colleagues away from issues which, once broached, could easily have led a majority of the Justices to adopt a position that would have put them on a collision course either with the other branches of the federal government, the states, or public opinion.

Controversies involving religion appear, however, to have sorely tested even Frankfurter's sense of self-restraint. In *Adamson v. California* (1947) he had rejected out of hand Justice Hugo Black's claim that the Fourteenth Amendment incorporated the entire Bill of Rights onto the states, and in another opinion, had forcefully stated that "the due process clause stands on its own bottom." Frankfurter seems to have had no problem, however, in agreeing with Justice Wiley Rutledge's dissent in *Everson*, despite the fact that Rutledge's opinion obviously sprang from the assumption that the First Amendment's prohibitions applied to the states via the Fourteenth Amendment. For Frankfurter, the religion clauses seemed to engender a very different response than any other section of the Bill of Rights. In fact, he was perhaps as great a defender of the nonestablishment principle as ever sat on the High Court. Unlike Douglas and Black, Frankfurter found the aid provided in *Everson* (1947) unconstitutional, and, unlike Douglas, he also rejected New York's released-time statute (*Zorach v. Clauson*–1952). Only Mr. Justice Robert Jackson—also an exponent of judicial self-restraint—was as consistent a defender of the Jeffersonian legacy.

Frankfurter's major contribution to the debate on the religion clauses came, however, on the issue of free exercise. On this, his stance can be more easily squared with his overall philosophy of judicial self-restraint, probably best summed up by James Bradley Thayer, Harvard law professor, who argued that judicial self-restraint means that a court can only hold a law unconstitutional and "disregard the Act when those who have the right to make laws have not merely made a mistake, but have made a very clear one,—so clear that it is not open to rational question."

Frankfurter's opportunity to express his position on free exercise came in the flag salute cases *Minersville School District v. Gobitis* (1940) and *West Virginia State Board of Education v. Barnette* (1943). Prompted by developments in Europe in the 1930s and supported by groups such as the American Legion, many states had adopted laws requiring public school children to participate in flag salute ceremonies as part of their school's opening exercises. This new practice posed an immediate problem to members of the Jehovah's Witnesses, who believed that the Biblical proscription against worshipping "graven images" forbade them from saluting the flag. The Witnesses already had been involved in several constitutional cases involving the free speech provision of the First Amendment. In fact, so active were the Jehovah's Witnesses before the Court that Mr. Justice Harlan Fiske Stone had once remarked that they should be given "an endowment" for their efforts in expanding the boundaries of the First Amendment.

The Witnesses' luck before the Court apparently ran out in *Gobitis* (1940), in which the Court, in an opinion by Justice Frankfurter with only Justices Jackson and Stone dissenting, upheld the flag salute requirement against the Witnesses' free exercise claim. The decision came as a hard blow to the sect, already unpopular because of the zeal with which they sought to spread their views. Now they were branded as being unpatriotic as well. The decision also came as a shock to much of the legal community, which had assumed that the Witnesses would prevail—they had won in the lower court. Three years later, the flag salute issue was again before the Court, but this time the result was different. Writing for a six-Justice majority, Justice Jackson overturned *Gobitis*, basing his decision, however, not on free exercise but on freedom of speech. Said Jackson:

> To sustain the compulsory flag salute we are required to say that a Bill of Rights which guards the individual's right to speak his own mind, left it open to public authorities to compel him to utter what is not in his mind.

Rejecting this position as foreign to the American system of government, Jackson, in his usual elegant and eloquent prose, concluded:

> If there is any fixed star in our constitutional constellation, it is that no official, high or petty, can prescribe what shall be orthodox in politics, nationalism, religion, or other matters of opinion or force citizens to confess by word or act their faith therein. If there are any circumstances which permit an exception, they do not now occur to us.

For his part, Frankfurter held firm, reiterating in even stronger language his *Gobitis* position. His memorable and moving dissent in *Barnette*, however, garnered only the votes of Justices Reed and Roberts. Ironically, despite Frankfurter's defeat in *Barnette*, the view he expressed there of the free exercise clause would prevail until *Sherbert v. Verner* (1963). Such was the intellectual power of the Justice who has been called "the Emily Post of the Court."

Also interesting is the fact that free exercise is one issue—one among very few—on which Black and Frankfurter, so often bitter adversaries, appear to have agreed. Neither was willing to read the free exercise provision of the First Amendment as protecting anything other than belief. Practice or ritual were subject to state regulation, to the will of the majority.

For Black, the literalist, such a rendering of the free exercise clause was obviously necessary; otherwise Chief Justice Morrison Waite's dire warning from *Reynolds v. United States* (1878)—the Mormon polygamy case—would come true. Waite had argued in *Reynolds* that "[t]o permit this would be to make the professed doctrines of religious belief superior to the law of the land, and in effect to permit every citizen to become a law unto himself." Only by limiting free exercise to belief could Black also protect his absolutist scruples and be able to continue to say: "no law means no law."

For Frankfurter, ever mindful of his foreign birth and his status as a religious minority member himself, the issue of religion—both establishment and free exercise—presents the curious example of an almost absolutist position taken by a judge who generally was inclined to balance conflicting claims and to rule on each case on its own merits.

WEST VIRGINIA STATE BOARD OF EDUCATION ET AL. *v.* BARNETTE ET AL.

APPEAL FROM THE DISTRICT COURT OF THE UNITED STATES
FOR THE SOUTHERN DISTRICT OF WEST VIRGINIA

319 U.S. 624 (1943)

MR. JUSTICE FRANKFURTER, dissenting:

One who belongs to the most vilified and persecuted minority in history is not likely to be insensible to the freedoms guaranteed by our Constitution. Were my purely personal attitude relevant I should wholeheartedly associate myself with the general libertarian views in the Court's opinion, representing as they do the thought and action of a lifetime. But as judges we are neither Jew nor Gentile, neither Catholic nor agnostic. We owe equal attachment to the Constitution and are equally bound by our judicial obligations whether we derive our citizenship from the earliest or the latest immigrants to these shores. As a member of this Court I am not justified in writing my private notions of policy into the Constitution, no matter how deeply I may cherish them or how mischievous I may deem their disregard.

* * * * *

Not so long ago we were admonished that "the only check upon our own exercise of power is our own sense of self-restraint. For the removal of unwise laws from the statute books appeal lies not to the courts but to the ballot and to the processes of democratic government."

United States v. *Butler,* 297 U. S. 1, 79 (dissent)

* * * * *

Conscientious scruples, all would admit, cannot stand against every legislative compulsion to do positive acts in conflict with such scruples. We have been told that such compulsions override religious scruples only as to major concerns of the state. But the determination of what is major and what is minor itself raises questions of policy. For the way in which men equally guided by reason appraise importance goes to the very heart of policy. Judges should be very diffident in setting their judgment against that of a state in determining what is and what is not a major concern, what means are appropriate to proper ends, and what is the total social cost in striking the balance of imponderables.

What one can say with assurance is that the history out of which grew constitutional provisions for religious equality and the writings of the great exponents of religious freedom—Jefferson, Madison, John Adams, Benjamin Franklin—are totally wanting in justification for a claim by dissidents of exceptional immunity from civic measures of general applicability, measures not in fact disguised assaults upon such dissident views. The great leaders of the American Revolution were determined to remove political support from every religious establishment. They put on an equality the different religious sects—Episcopalians, Presbyterians, Catholics, Baptists, Methodists, Quakers, Huguenots—which, as dissenters, had been under the heel of the various orthodoxies that prevailed in different colonies. So far as the state was concerned, there was to be neither orthodoxy nor heterodoxy. And so Jefferson and those who followed him wrote guaranties of religious freedom into our constitutions. Religious minorities as well as religious majorities were to be equal in the eyes of the political state. But Jefferson and the others also knew that minorities may disrupt society. It never would have occurred to them to write into the Constitution the subordination of the general civil authority of the state to sectarian scruples.

The constitutional protection of religious freedom terminated disabilities, it did not create new privileges. It gave religious equality, not civil immunity. Its essence is freedom from conformity to religious dogma, not freedom from conformity to law because of religious dogma. Religious loyalties may be exercised without hindrance from the state, not the state may not exercise that which except by leave of religious loyalties is within the domain of temporal power. Otherwise each individual could set up his own censor against obedience to laws conscientiously deemed for the public good by those whose business it is to make laws.

*　　*　　*　　*　　*

The essence of the religious freedom guaranteed by our Constitution is therefore this: no religion shall either receive the state's support or incur its hostility. Religion is outside the sphere of political government. This does not mean that all matters on which religious organizations or beliefs may pronounce are outside the sphere of government. Were this so, instead of the separation of church and state, there would be the subordination of the state on any matter deemed within the sovereignty of the religious conscience. Much that is the concern of temporal authority affects the spiritual interests of men. But it is not enough to strike down a non-discriminatory law that it may hurt or offend some dissident view. It would be too easy to cite numerous prohibitions and injunctions to which laws run counter if the variant interpretations of the Bible were made the tests of obedience to law. The validity of secular laws cannot be measured by their conformity to religious doctrines. It is only in a theocratic state that ecclesiastical doctrines measure legal right or wrong.

* * * * *

Parents have the privilege of choosing which schools they wish their children to attend. And the question here is whether the state may make certain requirements that seem to it desirable or important for the proper education of those future citizens who go to schools maintained by the states, or whether the pupils in those schools may be relieved from those requirements if they run counter to the consciences of their parents. Not only have parents the right to send children to schools of their own choosing but the state has no right to bring such schools "under a strict governmental control" or give "affirmative direction concerning the intimate and essential details of such schools, entrust their control to public officers, and deny both owners and patrons reasonable choice and discretion in respect of teachers, curriculum, and textbooks." *Farrington* v. *Tokushige*, 273 U. S. 284, 298. Why should not the state likewise have constitutional power to make reasonable provisions for the proper instruction of children in schools maintained by it?

* * * * *

There are other issues in the offing which admonish us of the difficulties and complexities that confront states in the duty of administering their local school systems. All citizens are taxed for the support of public schools although this Court has denied the right of a state to compel all children to go to such schools and has recognized the right of parents to send children to privately maintained schools. Parents who are dissatisfied with the public schools thus carry a double educational burden. Children who go to public school enjoy in many states derivative advantages such as free textbooks, free lunch, and free transportation in going to and from school. What of the claims for equality of treatment of those parents who, because of religious scruples, cannot send their children to public schools? What of the claim that if the right to send children to privately maintained schools is partly an exercise of religious conviction, to render effective this right it should be accompanied by equality of treatment by the state in supplying free textbooks, free lunch, and free transportation to children who go to private schools? What of the claim that such grants are offensive to the cardinal constitutional doctrine of separation of church and state?

These questions assume increasing importance in view of the steady growth of parochial schools both in number and in population. I am not borrowing trouble by adumbrating these issues nor am I parading horrible examples of the consequences of today's decision. I am aware that we must decide the case before us and not some other case. But that does not mean that a case is dissociated from the past and unrelated to the future.

* * * * *

It is probably not accidental that only a year after Frankfurter's retirement in 1962 (and President John Kennedy's nomination of Arthur J. Goldberg as his successor) the secular regulation rule was dealt a harsh blow in *Sherbert v. Verner* (1963).

Mrs. Sherbert, a Seventh-day Adventist, had been denied unemployment benefits because she would not work on Saturdays. Her refusal to work on Saturday grew out of the teachings of her church that Saturday, the seventh day, was the Sabbath. The majority of the Court accepted her argument that this practice contravened her guarantee to free exercise (See Burger: "The New Free Exercise").

John Marshall Harlan, the younger Mr. Justice Harlan, dissented, along with Justice Byron White. His dissent clearly attests to his status as successor in Frankfurter's role on the Supreme Court.

SHERBERT v. VERNER ET AL., MEMBERS OF SOUTH CAROLINA EMPLOYMENT SECURITY COMMISSION, ET AL.

APPEAL FROM THE SUPREME COURT OF SOUTH CAROLINA

374 U. S. 398 (1963)

MR. JUSTICE HARLAN, whom MR. JUSTICE WHITE joins, dissenting.

Today's decision is disturbing both in its rejection of existing precedent and in its implications for the future.

* * * * *

. . . [T]he purpose of the legislature was to tide people over, and to avoid social and economic chaos, during periods when *work was unavailable*. But at the same time there was clearly no intent to provide relief for those who for purely personal reasons were or became *unavailable for work*.

* * * * *

What the Court is holding is that if the State chooses to condition unemployment compensation on the applicant's availability for work, it is constitutionally compelled to *carve out an exception*—and to provide benefits—for those whose unavailability is due to their religious convictions. Such a holding has particular significance in two respects.

First, despite the Court's protestations to the contrary, the decision necessarily overrules *Braunfeld* v. *Brown*, 366 U. S. 599, which held that it did not offend the "Free Exercise" Clause of the Constitution for a State to forbid a Sabbatarian to do business on Sunday. The secular purpose of the statute before us today is even clearer than that involved in *Braunfeld*.

* * * * *

. . . [T]he indirect financial burden of the present law is far less than that involved in *Braunfeld*. Forcing a store owner to close his business on Sunday may well have the effect of depriving him of a satisfactory livelihood if his religious convictions require him to close on Saturday as well.

* * * * *

Second, the implications of the present decision are far more troublesome than its apparently narrow dimensions would indicate at first glance. The meaning of today's holding, as already noted, is that the State must furnish unemployment benefits to one who is unavailable for work if the unavailability stems from the exercise of religious convictions. The State, in other words, must *single out* for financial assistance those whose behavior is religiously motivated, even though it denies such assistance to others whose identical behavior (in this case, inability to work on Saturdays) is not religiously motivated.

It has been suggested that such singling out of religious conduct for special treatment may violate the constitutional limitations on state action. See Kurland, Of Church and State and The Supreme Court, 29 U. of Chi. L. Rev. 1; *cf. Cammarano* v. *United States*, 358 U. S. 498, 515 (concurring opinion). My own view, however, is that at least under the circumstances of this case it would be a permissible accommodation of religion for the State, if it *chose* to do so, to create an exception to its eligibility requirements for persons like the appellant.

* * * * *

I cannot subscribe to the conclusion that the State is constitutionally *compelled* to carve out an exception to its general rule of eligibility in the present case. Those situations in which the Constitution may require special treatment on account of religion are, in my view, few and far between, and this view is amply supported by the course of constitutional litigation in this area. . . .

Such compulsion in the present case is particularly inappropriate in light of the indirect, remote, and insubstantial effect of the decision below on the exercise of appellant's religion and in light of the direct financial assistance to religion that today's decision requires.

For these reasons I respectfully dissent from the opinion and judgment of the Court.

Chapter 3 HUGO L. BLACK: ABSOLUTE SEPARATIONIST

The First Amendment's guarantees of religious freedom had been part of the Constitution for over one hundred and fifty years before the Court was finally required to give its interpretation of what the phrase "Congress shall make no laws respecting the establishment of religion . . . ." meant. Whether its voice would have been different had it first been heard in 1800 rather than in 1947 is a question best left to Monday morning quarterbacks. The fact is that it was New Jersey's Ewing Township plan, by which parents of children attending nonprofit private schools were reimbursed for the costs of transporting their children to and from school, that would produce the Court's first interpretation of the establishment clause.

That no case had come to the Court in the intervening years was not at all remarkable. Congress generally had been inactive in the area. There were potential issues (e.g., military chaplains, prayers in Congress), but few had stirred the fervor necessary for potential plaintiffs to be willing to incur the costs and risk possible scorn in order to bring their cases before the Supreme Court. *Bradfield v. Roberts* (1899) stands as the solitary exception. Justice Peckham's opinion in the case, however, is of little if any help in elucidating the meaning of the establishment clause. As for state legislation, *Barron v. Baltimore* (1833) had effectively blocked any challenges based on the First Amendment. The establishment clause, like the rest of the Bill of Rights, had been held by Chief Justice Marshall in *Barron* to apply only to the federal government. This position would begin to change, and then quite slowly, only in the years after *Gitlow v. New York* (1925), the landmark case that so quietly acknowledged that a guarantee of the Bill of Rights—in this particular case, freedom of speech—was indeed one of the individual liberties protected by the Fourteenth Amendment from state abridgement. Even without the limitation of *Barron*, the fact that almost all of the states had in their own constitution provisions modeled on the defeated Blaine Amendment of 1876 reduced significantly the potential number of cases involving state aid to religious institutions. For opponents of such aid, there was no need to go to the federal courts. State courts were handier and more sympathetic. Finally, the United States Supreme Court's narrow interpretation of the concept of "standing" in the years prior to *Flast v. Cohen* (1968) served as a further roadblock to those opposed to governmental support of religion.

Accordingly, Justice Black was able to craft his opinion on a constitutional tabula rasa and, in so doing, to fix the issues for the judges who could come after him. The immediate result of Black's opinion, in which four other Justices joined, was that the Ewing Township ordinance, enacted under the authority of a New Jersey statute, was held constitutional, and parents of children in religious schools were entitled to continuing compensation for the travel expenses of their children. Black contended that the First Amendment's establishment clause had been carried over onto the states by a decision of the Court only four years earlier, *Murdock v. Pennsylvania* (1943).

Clearly more important than the result, however, was the light in which the *Everson* opinion presented the history of the First Amendment's guarantees of religious liberty. Obviously, Madison had played a major role in the formulation of the phrases that were to find their way into the First Amendment, and Jefferson had been a seminal thinker on the subject of religious liberty. But others had played a role in shaping the First Amendment and, perhaps of more importance, in shaping American opinion on the subject. The Harvard historian Mark deWolfe Howe contributed mightily in his book *The Wilderness and the Garden* to restoring some appreciation of the role of Roger Williams in affecting American attitudes on the matter of religious liberty. Neither Williams nor any of these others, however, plays a role in shaping Black's opinion or those of the dissenting jurists. While they might sharply disagree on the outcome of the case, all who wrote accepted the primacy of Jefferson and Madison. It is to these two "Founding Fathers" and to their writings, all the Justices agree that one must turn in order to discern the true meaning of the religion clauses.

Also of significance relative to Black's opinion is the fact that the Justice, while upholding the Ewing Township ordinance, made it quite clear that he saw it as "approach[ing] the verge" of unconstitutionality. To those hoping for more government aid to religious schools, this provided little comfort, particularly since the four dissenting Justices—Jackson, Frankfurter, Rutledge, and Burton—had seen even reimbursement of bus fares as being in violation of the Constitution.

Black's opinion has remained the precedential foundation stone upon which all subsequent establishment clause cases have rested, some more solidly, to be sure, than others. Black offered the first definition of the establishment clause—a standard that Justice Stevens, in his opinion in *Wolman v. Walter* (1977) considers to be as valuable today as when it was first crafted. It identified "neutrality" as being at the heart of the First Amendment, and laid the basis for the "secular purpose" test that can be found as the first prong of the Court's current three-pronged test (See Powell: "The Three and One-Half Pronged Test").

EVERSON v. BOARD OF EDUCATION OF THE TOWNSHIP OF EWING ET AL.

APPEAL FROM THE SUPREME COURT OF ERRORS AND APPEALS OF NEW JERSEY

330 U. S. 1 (1947)

MR. JUSTICE BLACK delivered the opinion of the Court.

A New Jersey statute authorizes its local school districts to make rules and contracts for the transportation of children to and from schools. The appellee, a township board of education, acting pursuant to this statute, authorized reimbursement to parents of money expended by them for the bus transportation of their children on regular busses operated by the public transportation system. Part of this money was for the payment of transportation of some children in the community to Catholic parochial schools. These church schools give their students, in addition to secular education, regular religious instruction conforming to the religious tenets and modes of worship of the Catholic Faith. The superintendent of these schools is a Catholic priest.

The appellant, in his capacity as a district taxpayer, filed suit in a state court challenging the right of the Board to reimburse parents of parochial school students. He contended that the statute and the resolution passed pursuant to it violated both the State and the Federal Constitutions. That court held that the legislature was without power to authorize such payment under the state constitution. 132 N. J. L. 98, 39 A. 2d 75. The New Jersey Court of Errors and Appeals reversed, holding that neither the statute nor the resolution passed pursuant to it was in conflict with the State constitution or the provisions of the Federal Constitution in issue. 133 N. J. L. 350, 44 A. 2d 333. The case is here on appeal under 28 U. S. C. § 344 (a).

Since there has been no attack on the statute on the ground that a part of its language excludes children attending private schools operated for profit from enjoying State payment for their transportation, we need not consider this exclusionary language; it has no relevancy to any constitutional question here presented.

* * * * *

The only contention here is that the state statute and the resolution, insofar as they authorized reimbursement to parents of children attending parochial schools, violate the Federal Constitution in these two respects, which to some extent overlap. *First.* They authorize the State to take by taxation the private property of some and bestow it upon others, to be used for their own private purposes. This, it is alleged, violates the due process clause of the Fourteenth Amendment. *Second.* The statute and the resolution forced inhabitants to pay taxes to help support and maintain schools which are dedicated to, and which regularly teach, the Catholic Faith. This is alleged to be a use of state power to support church schools contrary to the prohibition of the First Amendment which the Fourteenth Amendment made applicable to the states.

First. The due process argument . . . :

It is much too late to argue that legislation intended to facilitate the opportunity of children to get a secular education serves no public purpose. *Cochran* v. *Louisiana State Board of Education*, 281 U. S. 370. . . .

The same thing is no less true of legislation to reimburse needy parents, or all parents, for payment of the fares of their children so that they can ride in public busses to and from schools rather than run the risk of traffic and other hazards incident to walking or "hitchhiking."

* * * * *

Second. The New Jersey statute is challenged as a "law respecting an establishment of religion." The First Amendment, as made applicable to the states by the Fourteenth, *Murdock v. Pennsylvania*, 319 U. S. 105, commands that a state "shall make no law respecting an establishment of religion or prohibiting the free exercise thereof. . . ."

* * * * *

Whether this New Jersey law is one respecting an "establishment of religion" requires an understanding of the meaning of that language, particularly with respect to the imposition of taxes. Once again, therefore, it is not inappropriate briefly to review the background and environment of the period in which that constitutional language was fashioned and adopted.

A large proportion of the early settlers of this country came here from Europe to escape the bondage of laws which compelled them to support and attend government-favored churches. The centuries immediately before and contemporaneous with the colonization of America had been filled with turmoil, civil strife, and persecutions, generated in large part by established sects determined to maintain their absolute political and religious supremacy. With the power of government supporting them, at various times and places, Catholics had persecuted Protestants, Protestants had persecuted Catholics, Protestant sects had persecuted other Protestant sects, Catholics of one shade of belief had persecuted Catholics of another shade of belief, and all of these had from time to time persecuted Jews.

* * * * *

These practices of the old world were transplanted to and began to thrive in the soil of the new America.

* * * * *

These practices became so commonplace as to shock the freedom-loving colonials into a feeling of abhorrence. The imposition of taxes to pay ministers' salaries and to build and maintain churches and church property aroused their indignation. It was these feelings which found expression in the First Amendment. No one locality and no one group throughout the Colonies can rightly be given entire credit for having aroused the sentiment that culminated in adoption of the Bill of Rights' provisions embracing religious liberty. But Virginia, where the established church had achieved a dominant influence in political affairs and where many excesses attracted wide public attention, provided a great stimulus and able leadership for the movement.

* * * * *

The movement toward this end reached its dramatic climax in Virginia in 1785–86 when the Virginia legislative body was about to renew Virginia's tax levy for the support of the established church. Thomas Jefferson and James Madison led the fight against this tax. Madison wrote his great Memorial and Remonstrance against the law. In it, he eloquently argued that a true religion did not need the support of law; that no person, either believer or non-believer, should be taxed to support a religious institution of any kind; that the best interest of a society required that the minds of men always be wholly free; and that cruel persecutions were the inevitable result of government-established religions. Madison's Remonstrance received strong suppport throughout Virginia, and the Assembly postponed consideration of the proposed tax measure until its next session. When the proposal came up for consideration at that session, it not only died in committee, but the Assembly enacted the famous "Virginia Bill for Religious Liberty" originally written by Thomas Jefferson. The preamble to that Bill stated among other things that

> "Almighty God hath created the mind free; that all attempts to influence it by temporal punishments or burthens, or by civil incapacitations, tend only to beget habits of hypocrisy and meanness and are a departure from the plan of the Holy author of our religion, who being Lord both of body and mind, yet chose not to propagate it by coercions on either . . . ; that to compel a man to furnish contributions of money for the propagation of opinions which he disbelieves, is sinful and tyrannical; that even the forcing him to support this or that teacher of his own religious persuasion, is depriving him of the comfortable liberty of giving his contributions to the particular pastor, whose morals he would make his pattern. . . ."

And the statute itself enacted

> "That no man shall be compelled to frequent or support any religious worship, place, or ministry whatsoever, nor shall be enforced, restrained, molested, or burthened in his body or goods, nor shall otherwise suffer on account of his religious opinions or belief. . . ."

This Court has previously recognized that the provisions of the First Amendment, in the drafting and adoption of which Madison and Jefferson played such leading roles, had the same objective and were intended to provide the same protection against governmental intrusion on religious liberty as the Virginia statute. *Reynolds* v. *United States, supra* at 164.

*   *   *   *   *

The meaning and scope of the First Amendment, preventing establishment of religion or prohibiting the free exercise thereof, in the light of its history and the evils it was designed forever to suppress, have been several times elaborated by the decisions of this Court prior to the application of the First Amendment to the states by the Fourteenth. The broad meaning given the Amendment by these earlier cases has been accepted by this Court in its decisions concerning an individual's religious freedom rendered since the Fourteenth Amendment was interpreted to make the prohibitions of the First applicable to state action abridging religious freedom. There is every reason to give the same application and broad interpretation to the "establishment of religion" clause.

*   *   *   *   *

The "establishment of religion" clause of the First Amendment means at least this: Neither a state nor the Federal Government can set up a church. Neither can pass laws which aid one religion, aid all religions, or prefer one religion over another. Neither can force nor influence a person to go to or to remain away from church against his will or force him to profess a belief or disbelief in any religion. No person can be punished for entertaining or professing religious beliefs or disbeliefs, for church attendance or non-attendance. No tax in any amount, large or small, can be levied to support any religious activities or institutions, whatever they may be called, or whatever form they may adopt to teach or practice religion. Neither a state nor the Federal Government can, openly or secretly, participate in the affairs of any religious organizations or groups and *vice versa.* In the words of Jefferson, the clause against establishment of religion by law was intended to erect "a wall of separation between church and State." *Reynolds* v. *United States, supra* at 164.

We must consider the New Jersey statute in accordance with the foregoing limitations imposed by the First Amendment. But we must not strike that state statute down if it is within the State's constitutional power even though it approaches the verge of that power. See *Interstate Ry.* v. *Massachusetts*, Holmes, J., *supra* at 85, 88. New Jersey cannot consistently with the "establishment of religion" clause of the First Amendment contribute tax-raised funds to the support of an institution which teaches the tenets and faith of any church. On the other hand, other language of the amendment commands that New Jersey cannot hamper its citizens in the free exercise of their own religion. Consequently, it cannot exclude individual Catholics, Lutherans, Mohammedans, Baptists, Jews, Methodists, Non-believers, Presbyterians, or the members of any other faith, *because of their faith or lack of it*, from receiving the benefits of public welfare legislation. While we do not mean to intimate that a state could not provide transportation only to children attending public schools, we must be careful, in protecting the citizens of New Jersey against state-established churches, to be sure that we do not inadvertently prohibit New Jersey from extending its general state law benefits to all its citizens without regard to their religious belief.

Measured by these standards, we cannot say that the First Amendment prohibits New Jersey from spending tax-raised funds to pay the bus fares of parochial school pupils as a part of a general program under which it pays the fares of pupils attending public and other schools. It is undoubtedly true that children are helped to get to church schools. There is even a possibility that some of the children might not be sent to the church schools if the parents were compelled to pay their children's bus fares out of their own pockets when transportation to a public school would have been paid for by the State. The same possibility exists where the state requires a local transit company to provide reduced fares to school children including those attending parochial schools, or where a municipally owned transportation system undertakes to carry all school children free of charge. Moreover, state-paid policemen, detailed to protect children going to and from church schools from the very real hazards of traffic, would serve much the same purpose and accomplish much the same result as state provisions intended to guarantee free transportation of a kind which the state deems to be best for the school children's welfare. And parents might refuse to risk their children to the serious danger of traffic accidents going to and from parochial schools, the approaches to which were not protected by policemen. Similarly, parents might be reluctant to permit their children to attend schools which the state had cut off from such general government services as ordinary police and fire protection, connections for sewage disposal, public highways and sidewalks. Of course, cutting off church schools from these services, so separate and so indisputably marked off from the religious function, would make it far more difficult for the schools to operate. But such is obviously not the purpose of the First Amendment. That Amendment requires the state to be a neutral in its relations with groups of religious believers and non-believers; it does not require the state to be their adversary. State power is no more to be used so as to handicap religions than it is to favor them

This Court has said that parents may, in the discharge of their duty under state compulsory education laws, send their children to a religious rather than a public school if the school meets the secular educational requirements which the state has power to impose. See *Pierce* v. *Society of Sisters*, 268 U. S. 510. It appears that these parochial schools meet New Jersey's requirements. The State contributes no money to the schools. It does not support them. Its legislation, as applied, does no more than provide a general program to help parents get their children, regardless of their religion, safely and expeditiously to and from accredited schools.

The First Amendment has erected a wall between church and state. That wall must be kept high and impregnable. We could not approve the slightest breach. New Jersey has not breached it here.

Affirmed.

Chapter 4 WILLIAM O. DOUGLAS: ACCOMMODATIONISM

Justice William O. Douglas's opinion for the Court in *Zorach v. Clauson* has been a constant source of amazement in the years since it was issued in 1952. Justice Robert Jackson had earlier savaged Black's opinion in *Everson* by remarking that the precedent it most reminded him of was "that of Julia who, according to Byron's reports, 'whispering "I will ne'er consent,"—consented.'" He now dismissed Douglas's reasoning in equally cavalier fashion, stating that it would "be more interesting to students of psychology and of the judicial processes than to students of constitutional law." Others have unkindly speculated that the Douglas opinion was colored by his lingering desire to run for President. (The Justice had been seriously considered for the Democratic nomination for Vice-President in 1944, and his name had been mentioned again in 1948 by anti-Truman Democrats.) His opinion a year earlier in *Dennis v. United States* probably gives the lie to that charge. Defending the free speech rights of Communists in 1951 was hardly the way to become President in the era of Joseph McCarthy. Whatever his reasons for penning the *Zorach* opinion, Justice Douglas must have winced on occasion when critics of his later opinions on church-state issues buttressed their arguments for aid by quoting, with a certain devilish delight, the Justice's soon-to-be-famous words from his *Zorach* opinion, "We are a religious people whose institutions presuppose a Supreme Being."

Zorach v. Clauson arose out of a New York City public school program that released students from classes so that they could go to churches or synagogues for religious instruction during regular school time. Only four years earlier, a nearly unanimous Court—only Justice Stanley Reed had dissented—had held another "released time" program unconstitutional. In *McCollum v. Board of Education* (1948), however, the program was run in public school classrooms during regular class hours. *McCollum* had raised much opposition for released time programs had much support in the late forties and early fifties as America began experiencing a mini–religious revival. This was particularly true for Protestants, who were beginning to conclude that Sunday School was not enough. It had attracted some Catholic support, though the Catholic position was still that Catholic children should attend Catholic schools. Interestingly, it was a prominent attorney who frequently represented the Archdiocese of New York, Charles H. Tuttle, who now appeared on behalf of the Greater New York Coordinating Committee on Released Time.

Zorach's importance to both Catholics and Protestants, as well as to others interested in the First Amendment, is not difficult to understand. In an area of constitutional law where few precedents existed at the time, the outcome of this case could affect many issues, not simply released time. Specifically, it could do much to answer questions as to the precise dimensions of Thomas Jefferson's wall of separation," raised by Justice Black's opinion in *Everson v. Board of Education* (1947).

Although the majority per Douglas upheld the New York City plan, the Court was as sharply divided as it had been in *Everson*, with those who saw a violation of the establishment clause again a minority. Among the dissenters this time was Douglas's closest ally on the Court, Hugo Black. Douglas's language must have been seen as a victory for those who had earlier been warned by Justice Black in *Everson* that they were close to the forbidden "abyss." Indeed, it ranks alongside *Pierce v. Society of Sisters* (1925), which upheld the right of private schools to exist; *Cochran v. Board of Education* (1930), which sustained Louisiana's provision of textbooks to parochial school children under the rubric of "child benefit"; and *Board of Education v. Allen* (1968), which permitted New York school boards to lend books to children attending religious schools as a victory for those who do not see the Constitution's proscription against "the establishment of religion" as prohibiting all types of aid to religiously affiliated institutions—aid programs that they would hereafter refer to as permissible "accommodations."

That the concept of "accommodation," much favored in the lexicon of pro-aid forces, comes from the Douglas opinion is more than a little ironic since *Zorach* was to be the last establishment clause case in which Justice Douglas did not find a violation of the First Amendment. Even more than Black, Douglas would henceforth do his best to build up "the wall between church and state"—fearful, like Jefferson, of the possibility that churches would seek to use the state to do their will.

ZORACH ET AL. v. CLAUSON ET AL., CONSTITUTING THE BOARD OF EDUCATION OF THE CITY OF NEW YORK, ET AL

343 U. S. 306 (1952)

MR. JUSTICE DOUGLAS delivered the opinion of the Court.

New York City has a program which permits its public schools to release students during the school day so that they may leave the school buildings and school grounds and go to religious centers for religious instruction or devotional exercises. A student is released on written request of his parents. Those not released stay in the classrooms. The churches make weekly reports to the schools, sending a list of children who have been released from public school but who have not reported for religious instruction.

This "released time" program involves neither religious instruction in public school classrooms nor the expenditure of public funds. All costs, including the application blanks, are paid by the religious organizations. The case is therefore unlike *McCollum* v. *Board of Education*, 333 U. S. 203, which involved a "released time" program from Illinois. In that case the classrooms were turned over to religious instructors. We accordingly held that the program violated the First Amendment which (by reason of the Fourteenth Amendment) prohibits the states from establishing religion or prohibiting its free exercise.

Appellants, who are taxpayers and residents of New York City and whose children attend its public schools, challenge the present law, contending it is in essence not different from the one involved in the *McCollum* case. Their argument, stated elaborately in various ways, reduces itself to this: the weight and influence of the school is put behind a program for religious instruction; public school teachers police it, keeping tab on students who are released; the classroom activities come to a halt while the students who are released for religious instruction are on leave; the school is a crutch on which the churches are leaning for support in their religious training; without the cooperation of the schools this "released time" program, like the one in the *McCollum* case, would be futile and ineffective. The New York Court of Appeals sustained the law against this claim of unconstitutionality. 303 N. Y. 161, 100 N. E. 2d 463. The case is here on appeal.

* * * * *

The briefs and arguments are replete with data bearing on the merits of this type of "released time" program.

[However,] those matters are of no concern here, since our problem reduces itself to whether New York by this sytem has either prohibited the "free exercise" of religion or has made a law "respecting an establishment of religion" within the meaning of the First Amendment.

It takes obtuse reasoning to inject any issue of the "free exercise" of religion into the present case. No one is forced to go to the religious classroom and no religious exercise or instruction is brought to the classrooms of the public schools. A student need not take religious instruction. He is left to his own desires as to the manner or time of his religious devotions, if any.

There is a suggestion that the system involves the use of coercion to get public school students into religious classrooms. There is no evidence in the record before us that supports that conclusion. The present record indeed tells us that the school authorities are neutral in this regard and do no more than release students whose parents so request. . . . Hence we put aside that claim of coercion both as respects the "free exercise" of religion and "an establishment of religion" within the meaning of the First Amendment.

Moreover, apart from that claim of coercion, we do not see how New York by this type of "released time" program has made a law respecting an establishment of religion within the meaning of the First Amendment. There is much talk of the separation of Church and State in the history of the Bill of Rights and in the decisions clustering around the First Amendment. See *Everson* v. *Board of Education*, 330 U. S. 1; *McCollum* v. *Board of Education, supra*. There cannot be the slightest doubt that the First Amendment reflects the philosophy that Church and State should be separated. And so far as interference with the "free exercise" of religion and an "establishment" of religion are concerned, the separation must be complete and unequivocal. The First Amendment within the scope of its coverage permits no exception; the prohibition is absolute. The First Amendment, however, does not say that in every and all respects there shall be a separation of Church and State. Rather, it studiously defines the manner, the specific ways, in which there shall be no concert or union or dependency one on the other. That is the common sense of the matter. Otherwise the state and religion would be aliens to each other—hostile, suspicious, and even unfriendly. Churches could not be required to pay even property taxes. Municipalities would not be permitted to render police or fire protection to religious groups. Policemen who helped parishioners into their places of worship would violate the Constitution. Prayers in our legislative halls; the appeals to the Almighty in the messages of the Chief Executive; the proclamations making Thanksgiving Day a holiday; "so help me God" in our courtroom oaths—these and all other references to the Almighty that run through our laws, our public rituals, our ceremonies would be flouting the First Amendment. A fastidious atheist or agnostic could even object to the supplication with which the Court opens each session: "God save the United States and this Honorable Court."

We would have to press the concept of separation of Church and State to these extremes to condemn the present law on constitutional grounds. The nullification of this law would have wide and profound effects. A Catholic student applies to his teacher for permission to leave the school during hours on a Holy Day of Obligation to attend a mass. A Jewish student asks his teacher for permission to be excused for Yom Kippur. A Protestant wants the afternoon off for a family baptismal ceremony. In each case the teacher requires parental consent in writing. In each case the teacher, in order to make sure the student is not a truant, goes further and requires a report from the priest, the rabbi, or the minister. The teacher in other words cooperates in a religious program to the extent of making it possible for her students to participate in it. Whether she does it occasionally for a few students, regularly for one, or pursuant to a systematized program designed to further the religious needs of all the students does not alter the character of the act.

We are a religious people whose institutions presuppose a Supreme Being. We guarantee the freedom to worship as one chooses. We make room for as wide a variety of beliefs and creeds as the spiritual needs of man deem necessary. We sponsor an attitude on the part of government that shows no partiality to any one group and that lets each flourish according to the zeal of its adherents and the appeal of its dogma. When the state encourages religious instruction or cooperates with religious authorities by adjusting the schedule of public events to sectarian needs, it follows the best of our traditions. For it then respects the religious nature of our people and accommodates the public service to their spiritual needs. To hold that it may not would be to find in the Constitution a requirement that the government show a callous indifference to religious groups. That would be preferring those who believe in no religion over those who do believe. Government may not finance religious groups nor undertake religious instruction nor blend secular and sectarian education nor use secular institutions to force one or some religion on any person. But we find no constitutional requirement which makes it necessary for government to be hostile to religion and to throw its weight against efforts to widen the effective scope of religious influence. The government must be neutral when it comes to competition between sects. It may not thrust any sect on any person. It may not make a religious observance compulsory. It may not coerce anyone to attend church, to observe a religious holiday, or to take religious instruction. But it can close its doors or suspend its operations as to those who want to repair to their religious sanctuary for worship or instruction. No more than that is undertaken here.

This program may be unwise and improvident from an educational or a community viewpoint. That appeal is made to us on a theory, previously advanced, that each case must be decided on the basis of "our own prepossessions." See *McCollum* v. *Board of Education, supra,* p. 238. Our individual preferences, however, are not the constitutional standard. The constitutional standard is the separation of Church and State. The problem, like many problems in constitutional law, is one of degree. See *McCollum* v. *Board of Education, supra*, p. 231.

In the *McCollum* case the classrooms were used for religious instruction and the force of the public school was used to promote that instruction. Here, as we have said, the public schools do no more than accommodate their schedules to a program of outside religious instruction. We follow the *McCollum* case. But we cannot expand it to cover the present released time program unless separation of Church and State means that public institutions can make no adjustments of their schedules to accommodate the religious needs of the people. We cannot read into the Bill of Rights such a philosophy of hostility to religion.

Chapter 5 POTTER STEWART: NO COERCION

    Appointment to the Supreme Court is a chastening event for even the most experienced. Oliver Wendell Holmes, Jr., upon coming to the High Court after twenty years on the Supreme Judicial Court of Massachusetts, claimed that he was a little concerned about the transition. How worried Holmes actually was, one is free to ponder on one's own. Clearly, however, both the Supreme Court's role within the American political system and the general respect that it enjoys in American society are unique—different from any other court in the land and, indeed, in the world. Thus, although some individuals come to the bench with a definite view as to how they will comport themselves on the High Court—Holmes surely did—many, if not most, do not.

    For this majority, then, it is not surprising to find that they generally position themselves in the middle of whatever extremes exist on the Court. Few, however, are found to maintain this stance during their entire tenure on the Court. Having established themselves and their judicial philosophies, they move either to the right or to the left. Chief Justice Warren is one of the best examples of this. Warren as the activist, liberal judge only emerged in the late fifties when, having studied both the Frankfurter and Black approaches (or possibly their personalities), he opted for the latter. On the current Court, John Paul Stevens is a good example of the pattern. Of late, Stevens seems to be abandoning the center and lining up more with Brennan and Marshall. Justice Byron White is yet another example, though White took a considerably longer time than normal to move from the center, taking a position that increasingly finds him allied with Burger, Rehnquist, and O'Connor on the Court's right wing.

Justice Potter Stewart was a notable exception to this rule. From the time of his appointment to the Court by President Eisenhower in 1958 to his surprise retirement in 1981, Stewart occupied a crucial center position on the Court, maintaining that apparently precarious role on both the Warren and Burger Courts. Given this, it is not surprising to find that Stewart's part in the controversies that have swirled about the religion clauses can also be characterized as centrist; at least it would appear to offer a middle way between the basically separationist philosophy that underlies most of the modern Court's decisions on religion and the proclaimed goals of the 1984 Republican Party platform. Stewart's stance is also unusual in that, unlike his colleagues (Justice Brennan being a possible exception), his stance is potentially applicable to cases arising under both the free exercise and establishment clauses—this despite the Justice's own rejection (in his *Schempp* dissent) of all efforts to fashion "a single constitutional standard of 'separation of church and state'" as likely to produce "a fallacious oversimplification."

Like the University of Chicago's distinguished Philip Kurland, Stewart's approach fuses the two clauses. For Stewart, the first and foremost goal of both is to prohibit governmental coercion in the realm of religious belief or behavior. Only when government coerces, in Stewart's view, does it violate the neutrality that the Court has declared to constitute the very heart of these First Amendment guarantees.

Stewart's philosophy on this subject was first fully presented in the public school prayer cases, generally classified as involving the establishment clause. It appears as well in cases more frequently categorized as involving free exercise, such as *Sherbert v. Verner* (1963). It also would seem to explain the Justice's rejection of the use of tax-supported programs designed to benefit religious schools, since tax monies are hardly raised without some degree of coercion.

Stewart was the Court's only dissenter in the 1963 Supreme Court decision of *School District v. Schempp* and the companion case of *Murray v. Curlett*. Whether Chief Justice Burger and Associate Justice Rehnquist—two members of the current Court who are generally conceded to be less than sympathetic to the *Schempp* philosophy—will utilize Stewart's approach as a means by which to advance their own goals remains to be seen, as the Court readies itself to face what may be a long string of cases involving "silent meditation."

Schempp arose out of a challenge to a Pennsylvania statute that required that "At least ten verses from the Holy Bible shall be read, without comment, at the opening of each school day," providing further that "Any child shall be excused from such

Bible reading, or attending such Bible reading, upon the written request of his parent or guardian.'' For Justice Tom Clark, who wrote the opinion of the Court in this case, the facts in *Schempp* and *Murray* bespoke a clear violation of "the wholesome 'neutrality'" on which the Court had based its previous decisions, and he warned that "the breach of neutrality that is today a trickling stream may all too soon become a raging torrent. . . ."

To this colorful portrayal of the facts, Justice Stewart replied in solo dissent:

SCHOOL DISTRICT OF ABINGTON TOWNSHIP
PENNSYLVANIA, ET AL. *v.* SCHEMPP, ET AL.

374 U. S. 303 (1963)

MR. JUSTICE STEWART, dissenting.

I think the records in the two cases before us are so fundamentally deficient as to make impossible an informed or responsible determination of the constitutional issues presented. Specifically, I cannot agree that on these records we can say that the Establishment Clause has necessarily been violated. But I think there exist serious questions under both that provision and the Free Exercise Clause—insofar as each is imbedded in the Fourteenth Amendment—which require the remand of these cases for the taking of additional evidence.

I.

The First Amendment declares that "Congress shall make no law respecting an establishment of religion, or prohibiting the free exercise thereof. . . ." It is, I think, a fallacious oversimplification to regard these two provisions as establishing a single constitutional standard of "separation of church and state," which can be mechanically applied in every case to delineate the required boundaries between government and religion. We err in the first place if we do not recognize, as a matter of history and as a matter of the imperatives of our free society, that religion and government must necessarily interact in countless ways. Secondly, the fact is that while in many contexts the Establishment Clause and the Free Exercise Clause fully complement each other, there are areas in which a doctrinaire reading of the Establishment Clause leads to irreconcilable conflict with the Free Exercise Clause.

A single obvious example should suffice to make the point. Spending federal funds to employ chaplains for the armed forces might be said to violate the Establishment Clause. Yet a lonely soldier stationed at some faraway outpost could surely complain that a government which did *not* provide him the opportunity for pastoral guidance was affirmatively prohibiting the free exercise of his religion. And such examples could readily be multiplied. The short of the matter is simply that the two relevant clauses of the First Amendment cannot accurately be reflected in a sterile metaphor which by its very nature may distort rather than illumine the problems involved in a particular case.

* * * * *

Since the *Cantwell* pronouncement in 1940, this Court has twice held invalid state laws on the ground that they were laws "respecting an establishment of religion" in violation of the Fourteenth Amendment. *McCollum* v. *Board of Education*, 333 U. S. 203; *Engel* v. *Vitale*, 370 U. S. 421. On the other hand, the Court has upheld against such a challenge laws establishing Sunday as a compulsory day of rest, *McGowan* v. *Maryland*, 366 U. S. 420, and a law authorizing reimbursement from public funds for the transportation of parochial school pupils. *Everson* v. *Board of Education*, 330 U. S. 1.

* * * * *

That the central value embodied in the First Amendment—and, more particularly, in the guarantee of "liberty" contained in the Fourteenth—is the safeguarding of an individual's right to free exercise of his religion has been consistently recognized.

* * * * *

It is this concept of constitutional protection embodied in our decisions which makes the cases before us such difficult ones for me. For there is involved in these cases a substantial free exercise claim on the part of those who affirmatively desire to have their children's school day open with the reading of passages from the Bible.

It has become accepted that the decision in *Pierce* v. *Society of Sisters*, 268 U. S. 510, upholding the right of parents to send their children to nonpublic schools, was ultimately based upon the recognition of the validity of the free exercise claim involved in that situation. It might be argued here that parents who wanted their children to be exposed to religious influences in school could, under *Pierce*, send their children to private or parochial schools. But the consideration which renders this contention too facile to be determinative has already been recognized by the Court: "Freedom of speech, freedom of the press, freedom of religion are available to all, not merely to those who can pay their own way." *Murdock* v. *Pennsylvania*, 319 U. S. 105, 111.

* * * * *

IV.

Our decisions make clear that there is no constitutional bar to the use of government property for religious purposes. On the contrary, this Court has consistently held that the discriminatory barring of religious groups from public property is itself a violation of First and Fourteenth Amendment guarantees. *Fowler v. Rhode Island*, 345 U. S. 67; *Niemotko v. Maryland*, 340 U. S. 268. A different standard has been applied to public school property, because of the coercive effect which the use by religious sects of a compulsory school system would necessarily have upon the children involved. *McCollum v. Board of Education*, 333 U. S. 203. But insofar as the *McCollum* decision rests on the Establishment rather than the Free Exercise Clause, it is clear that its effect is limited to religious instruction—to government support of proselytizing activities of religious sects by throwing the weight of secular authority behind the dissemination of religious tenets.

* * * * *

In the absence of evidence that the legislature or school board intended to prohibit local schools from substituting a different set of readings where parents requested such a change, we should not assume that the provisions before us—as actually administered—may not be construed simply as authorizing religious exercises, nor that the designations may not be treated simply as indications of the promulgating body's view as to the community's preference. We are under a duty to interpret these provisions so as to render them constitutional if reasonably possible.

* * * * *

In the absence of coercion upon those who do not wish to participate—because they hold less strong beliefs, other beliefs, or no beliefs at all—such provisions cannot, in my view, be held to represent the type of support of religion barred by the Establishment Clause. For the only support which such rules provide for religion is the withholding of state hostility—a simple acknowledgment on the part of secular authorities that the Constitution does not require extirpation for all expression of religious belief.

V.

I have said that these provisions authorizing religious exercises are properly to be regarded as measures making possible the free exercise of religion. But it is important to stress that, strictly speaking, what is at issue here is a privilege rather than a right. In other words, the question presented is not whether exercises such as those at issue here are constitutionally compelled, but rather whether they are constitutionally invalid. And that issue, in my view, turns on the question of coercion.

It is clear that the dangers of coercion involved in the holding of religious exercises in a schoolroom differ qualitatively from those presented by the use of similar exercises or affirmations in ceremonies attended by adults. Even as to children, however, the duty laid upon government in connection with religious exercises in the public schools is that of refraining from so structuring the school environment as to put any kind of pressure on a child to participate in those exercises; it is not that of providing an atmosphere in which children are kept scrupulously insulated from any awareness that some of their fellows may want to open the school day with prayer, or of the fact that there exist in our pluralistic society differences of religious belief.

*   *   *   *   *

Accommodation of religious differences on the part of the State, however, is not only permitted but required by that same Constitution.

The governmental neutrality which the First and Fourteenth Amendments require in the cases before us, in other words, is the extension of evenhanded treatment to all who believe, doubt, or disbelieve—a refusal on the part of the State to weight the scales of private choice. In these cases, therefore, what is involved is not state action based on impermissible categories, but rather an attempt by the State to accommodate those differences which the existence in our society of a variety of religious beliefs makes inevitable. The Constitution requires that such efforts be struck down only if they are proven to entail the use of the secular authority of government to coerce a preference among such beliefs.

It may well be, as has been argued to us, that even the supposed benefits to be derived from noncoercive religious exercises in public schools are incommensurate with the administrative problems which they would create. The choice involved, however, is one for each local community and its school board, and not for this Court. For, as I have said, religious exercises are not constitutionally invalid if they simply reflect differences which exist in the society from which the school draws its pupils. They become constitutionally invalid only if their administration places the sanction of secular authority behind one or more particular religious or irreligious beliefs.

To be specific, it seems to me clear that certain types of exercises would present situations in which no possibility of coercion on the part of secular officials could be claimed to exist. Thus, if such exercises were held either before or after the official school day, or if the school schedule were such that participation were merely one among a number of desirable alternatives, it could hardly be contended that the exercises did anything more than to provide an opportunity for the voluntary expression of religious belief. On the other hand, a law which provided for religious exercises during the school day and which contained no excusal provision would obviously be unconstitutionally coercive upon those who did not wish to participate. And even under a law containing an excusal provision, if the exercises were held during the school day, and no equally desirable alternative were provided by the school authorities, the likelihood that children might be under at least some psychological compulsion to participate would be great. In a case such as the latter, however, I think we would err if we *assumed* such coercion in the absence of any evidence.

VI.

Viewed in this light, it seems to me clear that the records in both of the cases before us are wholly inadequate to support an informed or responsible decision.

* * * * *

What our Constitution indispensably protects is the freedom of each of us, be he Jew or Agnostic, Christian or Atheist, Buddhist or Freethinker, to believe or disbelieve, to worship or not worship, to pray or keep silent, according to his own conscience, uncoerced and unrestrained by government. It is conceivable that these school boards, or even all school boards, might eventually find it impossible to administer a system of religious exercises during school hours in such a way as to meet this constitutional standard—in such a way as completely to free from any kind of official coercion those who do not affirmatively want to participate.* But I think we must not assume that school boards so lack the qualities of inventiveness and good will as to make impossible the achievement of that goal.

I would remand both cases for further hearings.

*For example, if the record in the *Schempp* case contained proof (rather than mere prophecy) that the timing of morning announcements by the school was such as to handicap children who did not want to listen to the Bible reading, or that the excusal provision was so administered as to carry any overtones of social inferiority, then impermissible coercion would clearly exist.

The 1962–1963 court term gave Justice Stewart another opportunity to express his view on the religion clauses. South Carolina's Employment Security Commission had denied unemployment compensation benefits to Sherbert, a member of the Seventh-day Adventist church, because of her unwillingness to take work on Saturday due to religious scruples. Justice Stewart's concurrence was triggered by his belief that *Sherbert* did not square with the Court's earlier ruling in *Braunfeld v. Brown*, a case that upheld the conviction of an Orthodox Jew for opening his store in violation of Pennsylvania's Sunday Closing Law. He also believed that *Sherbert* was in conflict with the Court's recent establishment clause decisions.

SHERBERT v. VERNER ET AL., MEMBERS OF SOUTH CAROLINA EMPLOYMENT SECURITY COMMISSION, ET AL.

374 U.S. 398 (1963)

MR. JUSTICE STEWART, concurring in the result.

Although fully agreeing with the result which the Court reaches in this case, I cannot join the Court's opinion. This case presents a double-barreled dilemma, which in all candor I think the Court's opinion has not succeeded in papering over. The dilemma ought to be resolved.

* * * * *

I am convinced that no liberty is more essential to the continued vitality of the free society which our Constitution guarantees than is the religious liberty protected by the Free Exercise Clause explicit in the First Amendment and imbedded in the Fourteenth. And I regret that on occasion, and specifically in *Braunfeld* v. *Brown, supra*, the Court has shown what has seemed to me a distressing insensitivity to the appropriate demands of this constitutional guarantee. By contrast I think that the Court's approach to the Establishment Clause has on occasion, and specifically in *Engel, Schempp* and *Murray*, been not only insensitive, but positively wooden, and that the Court has accorded to the Establishment Clause a meaning which neither the words, the history, nor the intention of the authors of that specific constitutional provision even remotely suggests.

But my views as to the correctness of the Court's decisions in these cases are beside the point here. The point is that the decisions are on the books. And the result is that there are many situations where legitimate claims under the Free Exercise Clause will run into head-on collision with the Court's insensitive and sterile construction of the Establishment Clause. The controversy now before us is clearly such a case.

* * * * *

To require South Carolina to so administer its laws as to pay public money to the appellant under the circumstances of this case is thus clearly to require the State to violate the Establishment Clause as construed by this Court. This poses no problem for me, because I think the Court's mechanistic concept of the Establishment Clause is historically unsound and constitutionally wrong. I think the process of constitutional decision in the area of the relationships between government and religion demands considerably more than the invocation of broad-brushed rhetoric of the kind I have quoted. And I think that the guarantee of religious liberty embodied in the Free Exercise Clause affirmatively requires government to create an atmosphere of hospitality and accommodation to the individual belief or disbelief. In short, I think our Constitution commands the positive protection by government of religious freedom—not only for a minority, however small—not only for the majority, however large—but for each of us.

* * * * *

The impact upon the appellant's religious freedom in the present case is considerably less onerous. [than in *Braunfeld*] We deal here not with a criminal statute, but with the particularized administration of South Carolina's Unemployment Compensation Act. Even upon the unlikely assumption that the appellant could not find suitable non-Saturday employment, the appellant at the worst would be denied a maximum of 22 weeks of compensation payments.

* * * * *

I think the *Braunfeld* case was wrongly decided and should be overruled, and accordingly I concur in the result reached by the Court in the case before us.

In cases involving aid to religious schools, an issue which became a regular staple of the Court in the seventies, Stewart could be counted as a solid supporter of those who saw such programs as violating the Constitution's prohibition against establishment. On the one occasion that Stewart wrote for the Court, although not a majority of the Court, his phrasing seems to reflect his continued concern that decisions involving establishment not be made in isolation from free exercise questions and vice versa. The opinion is from *Meek v. Pittenger*, a 1973 case that involved a multifaceted package of services that the Commonwealth of Pennsylvania had adopted to help students in religious and other private schools.

MEEK ET AL. *v.* PITTENGER, SECRETARY OF EDUCATION, ET AL.

421 U.S. 349

APPEAL FROM THE UNITED STATES DISTRICT COURT FOR THE EASTERN DISTRICT OF PENNSYLVANIA

No. 73–1765 Argued February 19, 1975—Decided May 19, 1975

MR. JUSTICE STEWART announced the judgment of the Court and delivered the opinion of the Court (Parts I, II, IV, and V), together with an opinion (Part III), in which MR. JUSTICE BLACKMUN and MR. JUSTICE POWELL, joined.

This case requires us to determine once again whether a state law providing assistance to nonpublic, church-related, elementary and secondary schools is constitutional under the Establishment Clause of the First Amendment, made applicable to the States by the Fourteenth Amendment. *Murdock* v. *Pennsylvania*, 319 U. S. 105, 108; *Cantwell* v. *Connecticut*, 310 U. S. 296, 303.

*   *   *   *   *

In judging the constitutionality of the various forms of assistance authorized by Acts 194 and 195, the District Court applied the three-part test that has been clearly stated, if not easily applied, by this Court in recent Establishment Clause cases. See, *e. g., Committee for Public Education & Religious Liberty* v. *Nyquist*, 413 U. S. 756, 772–773; *Lemon* v. *Kurtzman*, 403 U. S. 602, 612–613. First, the statute must have a secular legislative purpose. *E. g., Epperson* v. *Arkansas*, 393, U.S. 97. Second, it must have a "primary effect" that neither advances nor inhibits religion. *E. g., School District of Abington Township* v. *Schempp*, 374 U. S. 203. Third, the statute and its administration must avoid excessive government entanglement with religion. *E. g., Walz* v. *Tax Comm'n*, 397 U. S. 664.

These tests constitute a convenient, accurate distillation of this Court's efforts over the past decades to evaluate a wide range of governmental action challenged as violative of the constitutional prohibition against laws "respecting an establishment of religion," and thus provide the proper framework of analysis for the issues presented in the case before us. It is well to emphasize, however, that the tests must not be viewed as setting the precise limits to the necessary constitutional inquiry, but serve only as guidelines with which to identify instances in which the objectives of the Establishment Clause have been impaired. See *Tilton* v. *Richardson*, 403 U. S. 672, 677–678 (plurality opinion of BURGER, C. J.).

Primary among the evils against which the Establishment Clause protects "have been 'sponsorship, financial support, and active involvement of the sovereign in religious activity.' *Walz* v. *Tax Comm'n, supra,* at 668; *Lemon* v. *Kurtzman, supra,* at 612." *Committee for Public Education & Religious Liberty* v. *Nyquist, supra,* at 772. The Court has broadly stated that "[n]o tax in any amount, large or small, can be levied to support any religious activities or institutions, whatever they may be called, or whatever form they may adopt to teach or practice religion." *Everson* v. *Board of Education*, 330 U. S. 1, 16. But it is clear that not all legislative programs that provide indirect or incidental benefit to a religious institution are prohibited by the Constitution. See *Zorach* v. *Clauson*, 343 U. S. 306, 312; *Lemon* v. *Kurtzman, supra,* at 614. "The problem, like many problems in constitutional law, is one of degree." *Zorach* v. *Clauson, supra,* at 314.

Chapter 6 WILLIAM J. BRENNAN: THE *SHERBERT* AND *SCHEMPP* TESTS

William J. Brennan, the third of Eisenhower's six appointees to the Supreme Court, reached the High Court in part because of religion, specifically, because of Eisenhower's desire in the Presidental election year of 1956 to restore the Court's traditionally Catholic seat. This customary seat dates back to President William McKinley's appointment of Joseph McKenna in 1898; it had lapsed in 1948 when President Harry Truman picked Attorney General Tom Clark to replace Justice Frank Murphy.

Next to the appointment of Earl Warren, the Brennan choice was the most significant of Eisenhower's six Supreme Court nominations. On the Court, Brennan quickly emerged as a key figure, second only to the Chief Justice in fashioning what would become known as the Warren Court Revolution and arguably even more important than Associate Justice Hugo Black. (Black's unique judicial philosophy—though he was generally a supporter of the Warren Court—forced him sometimes to part company, particularly at the end of the Warren Era, with the liberal activist bloc of Warren, Douglas, Brennan, Fortas, and Marshall.) A 1970 survey substantiates this characterization of Brennan, finding the New Jerseyite to rank with the ''near great'' among the ninety-six Justices who had served up to then on the United States Supreme Court.

Probably the single most important decision of Brennan's career will be *Baker v. Carr* (1961), the first of the Warren Court's reapportionment decisions—a decision that plunged the Court into Felix Frankfurter's feared "political thicket," and which ranks, among the Warren Court rulings, second only to the Chief Justice's own opinion in *Brown v. Board of Education* (1954) in the scope of its impact upon American society.

Despite the importance of *Baker v. Carr*, Brennan's greatest contribution to the Court's constitutional jurisprudence comes in the area of the First Amendment. Since *Roth v. United States* (1957), Brennan has had the dubious distinction of being the Court's resident expert on obscenity, and (unlike Justice Black) Brennan, along with the other Justices, has viewed all the films. As the author of the Court's opinion in *Uphaus v. Wyman* (1959), he helped the Court to clean away one of the last remnants of the McCarthy era. Finally, Brennan's opinion in *New York Times Co. v. Sullivan* (1964) totally rewrote the law of libel in the United States, greatly expanding the freedom of the press to criticize public figures. It is a case that is still making headlines, as evidenced by the recent Westmoreland suit against CBS, Mike Wallace, and the producers of "Sixty Minutes."

His contributions to the debate over the meaning of the religion clauses have been equally important. Brennan, more than any of his colleagues, has tried to justify his decisions, to explain and to persuade rather than simply to cast down ultimatums to be obeyed by lesser mortals under the law.

Despite some trimming by Burger (See Burger: "Balancing Free Exercise Claims"), the Court's current interpretation of free exercise was fairly well set by Brennan's 1963 decision in *Sherbert v. Verner*. This opinion established for the first time that action (refusing to accept Saturday employment because of religious belief) that was bottomed solely on free exercise—and neither on free exercise coupled with freedom of speech, e.g., *Cantwell v. Connecticut* (1940), nor on free exercise joined to freedom of the press, e.g., *Murdock v. Pennsylvania* (1943)—was entitled to constitutional protection. His use of the equal protection concept of "compelling state interest" as the standard that a state must meet to justify a ". . . substantial infringement of appellant's First Amendment right" and his acknowledgement that "a rational relationship to some colorable state interest would [not] suffice . . ." is even more important, for it provided, in the normally hazy world of the religion clauses, a concept that has considerable precision because of its long and generally accepted use in equal protection cases.

Brennan's contribution to the establishment quandary has been equally thoughtful, despite some naysayers who argue that his lengthy concurrence in *Schempp* detracted needlessly from the opinion of the Court written by Justice Clark. The Brennan test unfortunately seems to have been generally overlooked in all the furor over the nonestablishment clause, particularly that kicked up by Clark's ruling in *Schempp* that compulsory prayers in public schools were not in accord with the "wholesome neutrality" required by the First Amendment.

Like the Court's official establishment test, Brennan's standard has three parts:

What the Framers meant to foreclose, and what our decisions under the Establishment Clause have forbidden, are those involvements of religious with secular institutions which (a) serve the essentially religious activities of religious institutions; (b) employ the organs of government for essentially religious purposes; or (c) use essentially religious means to serve governmental ends, where secular means would suffice. When the secular and religious institutions become involved in such a manner, there inhere in the relationship precisely those dangers—as much to church as to state—which the Framers feared would subvert religious liberty and the strength of a system of secular government.

Brennan reiterated this position in his concurrence in *Walz v. Tax Commission* (1970), which upheld the constitutionality of the property tax exemption for religious institutions against a challenge that claimed this required individuals" . . . indirectly . . . to make a contribution to religious bodies and thereby violates provisions prohibiting establishment of religion. . . ." Finally, in a college aid case, *Hunt v. McNair* (1973), Brennan, writing in dissent for himself and Justices Douglas and Marshall, employed his three-part test to show how the South Carolina plan ran afoul of the Constitution's prohibition.

Along with his willingness to explain his conclusions—to an extent unmatched by any of his colleagues—on the subject of church-state relations, Brennan also distinguishes himself by the fact that he seems to be the one Justice who exhibits equal enthusiasm for the defense of free exercise and the principle of nonestablishment. Only Justice Douglas could have been considered a true rival on this point. Black and Frankfurter seemed willing to forfeit free exercise in favor of nonestablishment and Stewart to forfeit nonestablishment for free exercise. White, Rehnquist, Burger, and O'Connor appear ready to back off from both free exercise and establishment when required by the occasion.

Brennan's arguments are, accordingly, well worth understanding, as the courts come face to face with a whole host of new First Amendment issues. The Roman Catholic church's opposition to homosexuals is already before two courts: in New York City, because of the New York archdiocese's refusal—joined by the Salvation Army—to sign a nondiscrimination pledge as a condition for eligibility to provide certain city-contracted services to the poor; in the District of Columbia, as a result of the refusal of Jesuit-run Georgetown University to grant school recognition to two student homosexual groups. Another old issue that may return is the question of taxing religion. The possibility that tax reformers just might succeed in simplifying federal taxes, and in the process eliminate the federal deduction for charitable contributions, raises the interesting question of whether an argument can successfully be made that such a deduction (at least for religious groups) is constitutionally mandated. With members of Catholic religions, traditionally exempted from federal income taxes, increasingly taking jobs outside Catholic institutions, should such an exemption continue? Already one lower federal court has ruled that it should not.

Reprinted below are excerpts from Brennan's opinion of the Court in *Sherbert*, as well as his concurrences in *Schempp* and *Walz*.

SHERBERT v. VERNER ET AL., MEMBERS OF SOUTH CAROLINA EMPLOYMENT SECURITY COMMISSION, ET AL.

374 U. S. 398 (1963)

APPEAL FROM THE SUPREME COURT OF SOUTH CAROLINA

MR. JUSTICE BRENNAN delivered the opinion of the Court.

Appellant, a member of the Seventh-day Adventist Church, was discharged by her South Carolina employer because she would not work on Saturday, the Sabbath Day of her faith. When she was unable to obtain other employment because from conscientious scruples she would not take Saturday work, she filed a claim for unemployment compensation benefits under the South Carolina Unemployment Compensation Act. That law provides that, to be eligible for benefits, a claimant must be "able to work and . . . available for work"; and, further, that a claimant is ineligible for benefits "[i]f . . . he has failed, without good cause . . . to accept available suitable work when offered him by the employment office or the employer. . . ." The appellee Employment Security Commission, in administrative proceedings under the statute, found that appellant's restriction upon her availability for Saturday work brought her within the provision disqualifying for benefits insured workers who fail, without good cause, to accept "suitable work when offered . . . by the employment office or the employer. . . . "The Commission's finding was sustained by the Court of Common Pleas for Spartanburg County. That court's judgment was in turn affirmed by the South Carolina Supreme Court, which rejected appellant's contention that, as applied to her, the disqualifying provisions of the South Carolina statute abridged her right to the free exercise of her religion secured under the Free Exercise Clause of the First Amendment through the Fourteenth Amendment. The State Supreme Court held specifically that appellant's ineligibility infringed no constitutional liberties because such a construction of the statute "places no restriction upon the appellant's freedom of religion nor does it in any way prevent her in the exercise of her right and freedom to observe her religious beliefs in accordance with the dictates of her conscience."

* * * * *

I.

The door of the Free Exercise Clause stands tightly closed against any governmental regulation of religious *beliefs* as such, *Cantrell* v. *Connecticut*, 310 U. S. 296, 303. Government may neither compel affirmation of a repugnant belief, *Torcaso* v. *Watkins*, 367 U. S. 488; nor penalize or discriminate against individuals or groups because they hold religious views abhorrent to the authorities, *Fowler* v. *Rhode Island*, 345 U. S. 67; nor employ the taxing power to inhibit the dissemination of particular religious views, *Murdock* v. *Pennsylvania*, 319 U. S. 105; *Follett* v. *McCormick*, 321 U. S. 573; *cf. Grosjean* v. *American Press Co.*, 297 U. S. 233. On the other hand, the Court has rejected challenges under the Free Exercise Clause to governmental regulation of certain overt acts prompted by religious beliefs or principles, for "even when the action is in accord with one's religious convictions, [it] is not totally free from legislative restrictions." *Braunfeld* v. *Brown*, 366 U. S. 599, 603. The conduct or actions so regulated have invariably posed some substantial threat to public safety, peace or order.

* * * * *

Plainly enough, appellant's conscientious objection to Saturday work constitutes no conduct prompted by religious principles of a kind within the reach of state legislation. If, therefore, the decision of the South Carolina Supreme Court is to withstand appellant's constitutional challenge, it must be either because her disqualification as a beneficiary represents no infringement by the State of her constitutional rights of free exercise, or because any incidental burden on the free exercise of appellant's religion may be justified by a "compelling state interest in the regulation of a subject within the State's constitutional power to regulate. . . ." *NAACP* v. *Button*, 371 U. S. 415, 438.

II.

We turn first to the question whether the disqualification for benefits imposes any burden on the free exercise of appellant's religion. We think it is clear that it does. In a sense the consequences of such a disqualification to religious principles and practices may be only an indirect result of welfare legislation within the State's general competence to enact; it is true that no criminal sanctions directly compel appellant to work a six-day week. But this is only the beginning, not the end, of our inquiry. For "[i]f the purpose or effect of a law is to impede the observance of one or all religions or is to discriminate invidiously between religions, that law is constitutionally invalid even though the burden may be characterized as being only indirect." *Braunfeld* v. *Brown, supra*, at 607. Here not only is it apparent that appellant's declared ineligibility for benefits derives solely from the practice of her religion, but the pressure upon her to forego that practice is unmistakable. The ruling forces her to choose between following the precepts of her religion and forfeiting benefits, on the one hand, and abandoning one of the precepts of her religion in order to accept work, on the other hand. Governmental imposition of such a choice puts the same kind of burden upon the free exercise of religion as would a fine imposed against appellant for her Saturday worship.

Nor may the South Carolina court's construction of the statute be saved from constitutional infirmity on the ground that unemployment compensation benefits are not appellant's "right" but merely a "privilege." It is too late in the day to doubt that the liberties of religion and expression may be infringed by the denial of or placing of conditions upon a benefit or privilege.

* * * * *

III.

We must next consider whether some compelling state interest enforced in the eligibility provisions of the South Carolina statute justifies the substantial infringement of appellant's First Amendment right. It is basic that no showing merely of a rational relationship to some colorable state interest would suffice; in this highly sensitive constitutional area, "[o]nly the gravest abuses, endangering paramount interests, give occasion for permissible limitation," *Thomas* v. *Collins*, 323 U. S. 516, 530. No such abuse or danger has been advanced in the present case. The appellees suggest no more than a possibility that the filing of fraudulent claims by unscrupulous claimants feigning religious objections to Saturday work might not only dilute the unemployment compensation fund but also hinder the scheduling by employers of necessary Saturday work. But that possibility is not apposite here because no such objection appears to have been made before the South Carolina Supreme Court, and we are unwilling to assess the importance of an asserted state interest without the views of the state court.

* * * * *

. . . [T]he state interest asserted in the present case is wholly dissimilar to the interests which were found to justify the less direct burden upon religious practices in *Braunfeld* v. *Brown, supra*. The Court recognized that the Sunday closing law which that decision sustained undoubtedly served "to make the practice of [the Orthodox Jewish merchants'] . . . religious beliefs more expensive," 366 U. S., at

605. But the statute was nevertheless saved by a countervailing factor which finds no equivalent in the instant case—a strong state interest in providing one uniform day of rest for all workers. That secular objective could be achieved, the Court found, only by declaring Sunday to be that day of rest. Requiring exemptions for Sabbatarians, while theoretically possible, appeared to present an administrative problem of such magnitude, or to afford the exempted class so great a competitive advantage, that such a requirement would have rendered the entire statutory scheme unworkable. In the present case no such justifications underlie the determination of the state court that appellant's religion makes her ineligible to receive benefits.

IV.

In holding as we do, plainly we are not fostering the "establishment" of the Seventh-day Adventist religion in South Carolina, for the extension of unemployment benefits to Sabbatarians in common with Sunday worshippers reflects nothing more than the governmental obligation of neutrality in the face of religious differences, and does not represent that involvement of religious with secular institutions which it is the object of the Establishment Clause to forestall. See *School District of Abington Township* v. *Schempp ante*, p. 203. Nor does the recognition of the appellant's right to unemployment benefits under the state statute serve to abridge any other person's religious liberties. Nor do we, by our decision today, declare the existence of a constitutional right to unemployment benefits on the part of all persons whose religious convictions are the cause of their unemployment. This is not a case in which an employee's religious convictions serve to make him a nonproductive member of society. . . . Finally, nothing we say today constrains the States to adopt any particular form or scheme of unemployment compensation. Our holding today is only that South Carolina may not constitutionally apply the eligibility provisions so as to constrain a worker to abandon his religious convictions respecting the day of rest. This holding but reaffirms a principle that we announced a decade and a half ago, namely that no State may "exclude individual Catholics, Lutherans, Mohammedans, Baptists, Jews, Methodists, Non-believers, Presbyterians, or the members of any other faith, *because of their faith, or lack of it*, from receiving the benefits of public welfare legislation." *Everson* v. *Board of Education*, 330 U. S. 1, 16.

In view of the result we have reached under the First and Fourteenth Amendments' guarantee of free exercise of religion, we have no occasion to consider appellant's claim that the denial of benefits also deprived her of the equal protection of the laws in violation of the Fourteenth Amendment.

The judgment of the South Carolina Supreme Court is reversed and the case is remanded for further proceedings not inconsistent with this opinion.

It is so ordered.

SCHOOL DISTRICT OF ABINGTON TOWNSHIP, PENNSYLVANIA, ET AL. *v.* SCHEMPP ET AL.

374 U. S. 203 (1963)

APPEAL FROM THE UNITED STATES DISTRICT COURT FOR THE EASTERN DISTRICT OF PENNSYLVANIA

MR. JUSTICE BRENNAN, concurring.

Almost a century and a half ago, John Marshall, in *M'Culloch* v. *Maryland*, enjoined: " . . . we must never forget, that it is a *constitution* we are expounding." 4 Wheat, 316, 407. The Court's historic duty to expound the meaning of the Constitution has encountered few issues more intricate or more demanding than that of the relationship between religion and the public schools. Since undoubtedly we are "a religious people whose institutions presuppose a Supreme Being," *Zorach* v. *Clauson*, 343 U. S. 306, 313 deep feelings are aroused when aspects of that relationship are claimed to violate the injunction of the First Amendment that government may make "no law respecting an establishment of religion, or prohibiting the free exercise thereof. . . ." Americans regard the public schools as a most vital civic institution for the preservation of a democratic system of government. It is therefore understandable that the constitutional prohibitions encounter their severest test when they are sought to be applied in the school classroom. Nevertheless it is this Court's inescapable duty to declare whether exercises in the public schools of the States, such as those of Pennsylvania and Maryland questioned here, are involvements of religion in public institutions of a kind which offends the First and Fourteenth Amendments.

. . . While our institutions reflect a firm conviction that we are a religious people, those institutions by solemn constitutional injunction may not officially involve religion in such a way as to prefer, discriminate against, or oppress, a particular sect or religion. Equally the Constitution enjoins those involvements of religious with secular institutions which (a) serve the essentially religious activities of religious institutions; (b) employ the organs of government for essentially religious purposes; or (c) use essentially religious means to serve governmental ends where secular means would suffice. . . .

I join fully in the opinion and the judgment of the Court. I see no escape from the conclusion that the exercises called in question in these two cases violate the constitutional mandate. The reasons we gave only last Term in *Engel* v. *Vitale*, 370 U. S. 421, for finding in the New York Regents' prayer an impermissible establishment of religion, compel the same judgment of the practices at bar. The involvement of the secular with the religious is no less intimate here; and it is constitutionally irrelevant that the State has not composed the material for the inspirational exercises presently involved. It should be unnecessary to observe that our holding does not declare that the First Amendment manifests hostility to the practice or teaching of religion, but only applies prohibitions incorporated in the Bill of Rights in recognition of historic needs shared by Church and State alike. While it is my view that not every involvement of religion in public life is unconstitutional, I consider the exercises at bar a form of involvement which clearly violates the Establishment Clause.

The importance of the issue and the deep conviction with which views on both sides are held seem to me to justify detailing at some length my reasons for joining the Court's judgment and opinion.

I.

The First Amendment forbids both the abridgment of the free exercise of religion and the enactment of laws "respecting an establishment of religion." The two clauses, although distinct in their objectives and their applicability, emerged together from a common panorama of history. The inclusion of both restraints upon the power of Congress to legislate concerning religious matters shows unmistakably that the Framers of the First Amendment were not content to rest the protection of religious freedom exclusively upon either clause.

* * * * *

. . . [A]n awareness of history and an appreciation of the aims of the Founding Fathers do not always resolve concrete problems. The specific question before us has, for example, aroused vigorous dispute whether the architects of the First Amendment— James Madison and Thomas Jefferson particularly—understood the prohibition against any "law respecting an establishment of religion" to reach devotional exercises in the public schools. It may be that Jefferson and Madison would have held such exercises to be permissible—although even in Jefferson's case serious doubt is suggested by his admonition against "putting the Bible and Testament into the hands of the children at an age when their judgments are not sufficiently matured for religious inquiries. . . ." But I doubt that their view, even if perfectly clear one way or the other, would supply a dispositive answer to the question presented by these cases. A more fruitful inquiry, it seems to me, is whether the practices here challenged threaten those consequences which the Framers deeply feared; whether, in short, they tend to promote that type of interdependence between religion and state which the First Amendment was designed to prevent. Our task is to translate "the majestic generalities of the Bill of Rights, conceived as part of the pattern of liberal government in the eighteenth century, into concrete restraints on officials dealing with the problem of the twentieth century. . . ." *West Virginia State Board of Education* v. *Barnette*, 319 U. S. 624, 639.

A too literal quest for the advice of the Founding Fathers upon the issues of these cases seems to me futile and misdirected for several reasons: First, on our precise problem the historical record is at best ambiguous, and statements can readily be found to support either side of the proposition. The ambiguity of history is understandable if we recall the nature of the problems uppermost in the thinking of the statesmen who fashioned the religious guarantees; they were concerned with far more flagrant intrusions of government into the realm of religion than any that our century has witnessed. . . .

Second, the structure of American education has greatly changed since the First Amendment was adopted. In the context of our modern emphasis upon public education available to all citizens, any views of the eighteenth century as to whether the exercises at bar are an "establishment" offer little aid to decision. Education, as the Framers knew it, was in the main confined to private schools more often than not under strictly sectarian supervision. Only gradually did control of education pass largely to public officials. It would, therefore, hardly be significant if the fact was that the nearly universal devotional exercises in the schools of the young Republic did not provoke criticism; even today religious ceremonies in church-supported private schools are constitutionally unobjectionable.

Third, our religious composition makes us a vastly more diverse people than were our forefathers. They knew differences chiefly among Protestant sects. Today the Nation is far more heterogeneous religiously, including as it does substantial minorities not only of Catholics and Jews but as well of those who worship according to no version of the Bible and those who worship no God at all. . . .

Whatever Jefferson or Madison would have thought of Bible reading or the recital of the Lord's Prayer in what few public schools existed in their day, our use of the history of their time must limit itself to broad purposes, not specific practices. By such a standard, I am persuaded, as is the Court, that the devotional exercises carried on in the Baltimore and Abington schools offend the First Amendment because they sufficiently threaten in our day those substantive evils the fear of which called forth the Establishment Clause of the First Amendment. It is "*a constitution* we are expounding," and our interpretation of the First Amendment must necessarily be responsive to the much more highly charged nature of religious questions in contemporary society.

*   *   *   *   *

II.

The exposition by this Court of the religious guarantees of the First Amendment has consistently reflected and reaffirmed the concerns which impelled the Framers to write those guarantees into the Constitution. It would be neither possible nor appropriate to review here the entire course of our decisions on religious questions. There emerge from those decisions, however, three principles of particular relevance to the issue presented by the cases at bar, and some attention to those decisions is therefore appropriate.

First. One line of decisions derives from contests for control of a church property or other internal ecclesiastical disputes. This line has settled the proposition that in order to give effect to the First Amendment's purpose of requiring on the part of all organs of government a strict neutrality toward theological questions, courts should not undertake to decide such questions.

* * * * *

Second. It is only recently that our decisions have dealt with the question whether issues arising under the Establishment Clause may be isolated from problems implicating the Free Exercise Clause.

* * * * *

Third. It is true, as the Court says, that the "two clauses [Establishment and Free Exercise] may overlap."

* * * * *

III.

No one questions that the Framers of the First Amendment intended to restrict exclusively the powers of the Federal Government. Whatever limitations that Amendment now imposes upon the States derive from the Fourteenth Amendment. The process of absorption of the religious guarantees of the First Amendment as protections against the States under the Fourteenth Amendment began with the Free Exercise Clause . . .

The absorption of the Establishment Clause has, however, come later and by a route less easily charted. It has been suggested, with some support in history, that absorption of the First Amendment's ban against congressional legislation "respecting an establishment of religion" is conceptually impossible because the Framers meant the Establishment Clause also to foreclose any attempt by Congress to disestablish the existing official state churches. Whether or not such was the understanding of the Framers and whether such a purpose would have inhibited the absorption of the Establishment Clause at the threshold of the Nineteenth Century are questions not dispositive of our present inquiry. For it is clear on the record of history that the last of the formal state establishments was dissolved more than three decades before the Fourteenth Amendment was ratified, and thus the problem of protecting official state churches from federal encroachments could hardly have been any concern of those who framed the post-Civil War Amendments. Any such objective of the First Amendment, having become historical anachronism by 1868, cannot be thought to have deterred the absorption of the Establishment Clause to any greater degree than it would, for example, have deterred the absorption of the Free Exercise Clause. . . .

It has also been suggested that the "liberty" guaranteed by the Fourteenth Amendment logically cannot absorb the Establishment Clause because that clause is not one of the provisions of the Bill of Rights which in terms protects a "freedom" of the individual. See Corwin, A Constitution of Powers in a Secular State (1951), 113–116. The fallacy in this contention, I think, is that it underestimates the role of the Establishment Clause as a co-guarantor, with the Free Exercise Clause, of religious liberty. . . .

Finally, it has been contended that absorption of the Establishment Clause is precluded by the absence of any intention on the part of the Framers of the Fourteenth Amendment to circumscribe the residual powers of the States to aid religious activities and institutions in ways which fell short of formal establishments. That argument relies in part upon the express terms of the abortive Blaine Amendment—proposed several years after the adoption of the Fourteenth Amendment—which would have added to the First Amendment a provision that "[n]o State shall make any law respecting an establishment of religion. . . ." Such a restriction would have been superfluous, it is said, if the Fourteenth Amendment had already made the Establishment Clause binding upon the States.

The argument proves too much, for the Fourteenth Amendment's protection of the free exercise of religion can hardly be questioned; yet the Blaine Amendment would also have added an explicit protection agaisnt state laws abridging that liberty. Even if we assume that the draftsmen of the Fourteenth Amendment saw no immediate connection between its protections against state action infringing personal liberty and the guarantees of the First Amendment, it is certainly too late in the day to suggest that their assumed inattention to the question dilutes the force of these constitutional gurantees in their application to the States. It is enough to conclude that the religious liberty embodied in the Fourteenth Amendment would not be viable if the Constitution were interpreted to forbid only establishments ordained by Congress.

The issue of what particular activities the Establishment Clause forbids the States to undertake is our more immediate concern. . . . It has rightly been said of the history of the Establishment Clause that "our tradition of civil liberty rests not only on the secularism of a Thomas Jefferson but also on the fervent sectarianism . . . of a Roger Williams." Freund, The Supreme Court of the United States (1961), 84.

Our decisions on questions of religious education or exercises in the public schools have consistently reflected this dual aspect of the Establishment Clause.

* * * * *

IV.

I turn now to the cases before us. The religious nature of the exercises here challenged seems plain. Unless *Engel* v. *Vitale* is to be overruled, or we are to engage in wholly disingenuous distinction, we cannot sustain these practices. Daily recital of the Lord's Prayer and the reading of passages of Scripture are quite as clearly breaches of the command of the Establishment Clause as was the daily use of the rather bland Regents' Prayer in the New York public schools. Indeed, I would suppose that, if anything, the Lord's Prayer and the Holy Bible are more clearly sectarian, and the present violations of the First Amendment consequently more serious. But the religious exercises challenged in these cases have a long history. And almost from the beginning, Bible reading and daily prayer in the schools have been the subject of debate, criticism by educators and other public officials, and proscription by courts and legislative councils. At the outset, then, we must carefully canvass both aspects of this history.

* * * * *

Statutory provision for daily religious exercises is, however, of quite recent origin. At the turn of this century, there was but one State—Massachusetts—which had a law making morning prayer or Bible reading obligatory. Statutes elsewhere either permitted such practices or simply left the question to local option. It was not until after 1910 that 11 more States, within a few years, joined Massachusetts in making one or both exercises compulsory. The Pennsylvania law with which we are concerned in the *Schempp* case, for example, took effect in 1913; and even the Rule of the Baltimore School Board involved in the *Murray* case dates only from 1905. In no State has there ever been a constitutional or statutory prohibition against the recital of prayers or the reading of Scripture, although a number of States have outlawed these practices by judicial decision or administrative order. What is noteworthy about the panoply of state and local regulations from which these cases emerge is the relative recency of the statutory codification of practices which have ancient roots, and the rather small number of States which have ever prescribed compulsory religious exercises in the public schools.

* * * * *

. . . [I]t is argued that however clearly religious may have been the origins and early nature of daily prayer and Bible reading, these practices today serve so clearly secular educational purposes that their religious attributes may be overlooked. I do not doubt, for example, that morning devotional exercises may foster better discipline in the classroom, and elevate the spiritual level on which the school day opens. The Pennsylvania Superintendent of Public Instruction, testifying by deposition in the *Schempp* case, offered his view that daily Bible reading "places upon the children or those hearing the reading of this, and the atmosphere which goes on in the reading . . . one of the last vestiges of moral value that we have left in our school system." . . .

It is not the business of this Court to gainsay the judgments of experts on matters of pedagogy. Such decisions must be left to the discretion of those administrators charged with the supervision of the Nation's public schools. The limited province of the courts is to determine whether the means which the educators have chosen to achieve legitimate pedagogical ends infringe the constitutional freedoms of the First Amendment.

* * * * *

Second, it is argued that the particular practices involved in the two cases before us are unobjectionable because they prefer no particular sect or sects at the expense of others. Both the Baltimore and Abington procedures permit, for example, the reading of any of several versions of the Bible, and this flexibility is said to ensure neutrality sufficiently to avoid the constitutional prohibition. One answer, which might be dispositive, is that any version of the Bible is inherently sectarian, else there would be no need to offer a system of rotation or alternation of versions in the first place, that is, to allow different sectarian versions to be used on different days. The sectarian character of the Holy Bible has been at the core of the whole controversy over religious practices in the public schools throughout its long and often bitter history. To vary the version as the Abington and Baltimore schools have done may well be less offensive than to read from the King James version every day, as once was the practice. But the result even of this relatively benign procedure is that majority sects are preferred in approximate proportion to their representation in the community and in the student body, while the smaller sects suffer commensurate discrimination. So long as the subject matter of the exercise is sectarian in character, these consequences cannot be avoided.

The argument contains, however, a more basic flaw. There are persons in every community—often deeply devout— to whom any version of the Judaeo-Christian Bible is offensive. There are others whose reverence for the Holy Scriptures demands private study or reflection and to whom public reading or recitation is sacrilegious, as one of the expert witnesses at the trial of the *Schempp* case explained. To such persons it is not the fact of using the Bible in the public schools, nor the content of any particular version, that is offensive, but only the *manner* in which it is used. For such persons, the anathema of public communion is even more pronounced when prayer is involved.

*   *   *   *   *

. . . Moreover, even if the Establishment Clause were oblivious to nonsectarian religious practices, I think it quite likely that the "common core" approach would be sufficiently objectionable to many groups to be foreclosed by the prohibitions of the Free Exercise Clause.

C.

A third element which is said to absolve the practices involved in these cases from the ban of the religious guarantees of the Constitution is the provision to excuse or exempt students who wish not to participate. Insofar as these practices are claimed to violate the Establishment Clause, I find the answer which the District Court gave after our remand of *Schempp* to be altogether dispositive:

> "The fact that some pupils, or theoretically all pupils, might be excused from attendance at the exercises does not mitigate the obligatory nature of the ceremony. . . . The exercises are held in the school buildings and perforce are conducted by and under the authority of the local school authorities and during school sessions. Since the statute requires the reading of the 'Holy Bible,' a Christian document, the practice, as we said in our first opinion, prefers the Christian religion. The record demonstrates that it was the intention of the General Assembly of the Commonwealth of Pennsylvania to introduce a religious ceremony into the public schools of the Commonwealth." 201 F. Supp., at 819.

Thus the short, and to me sufficient, answer is that the availability of excusal or exemption simply has no relevance to the establishment question, if it is once found that these practices are essentially religious exercises designed at least in part to achieve religious aims through the use of public school facilities during the school day.

The more difficult question, however, is whether the availability of excusal for the dissenting child serves to refute challenges to these practices under the Free Exercise Clause. While it is enough to decide these cases to dispose of the establishment questions, questions of free exercise are so inextricably interwoven into the history and present status of these practices as to justify disposition of this second aspect of the excusal issue. The answer is that the excusal procedure itself necessarily operates in such a way as to infringe the rights of free exercise of those children who wish to be excused. We have held in *Barnette* and *Torcaso*, respectively, that a State may require neither public school students nor candidates for an office of public trust to profess beliefs offensive to religious principles. By the same token the State could not constitutionally require a student to profess publicly his disbelief as the prerequisite to the exercise of his constitutional right of abstention.

* * * * *

V.

These considerations bring me to a final contention of the school officials in these cases: that the invalidation of the exercises at bar permits this Court no alternative but to declare unconstitutional every vestige, however slight, of cooperation or accommodation between religion and government. I cannot accept that contention. While it is not, of course, appropriate for this Court to decide questions not presently before it, I venture to suggest that religious exercises in the public schools present a unique problem. For not every involvement of religion in public life violates the Establishment Clause. Our decision in these cases does not clearly forecast anything about the constitutionality of other types of interdependence between religious and other public institutions.

Specifically, I believe that the line we must draw between the permissible and the impermissible is one which accords with history and faithfully reflects the understanding of the Founding Fathers. It is a line which the Court has consistently sought to mark in its decisions expounding the religious guarantees of the First Amendment. What the Framers meant to foreclose, and what our decisions under the Establishment Clause have forbidden, are those involvements of religious with secular institutions which (a) serve the essentially religious activities of religious institutions; (b) employ the organs of government for essentially religious purposes; or (c) use essentially religious means to serve governmental ends, where secular means would suffice. . . .

The line between permissible and impermissible forms of involvement between government and religion has already been considered by the lower federal and state courts. I think a brief survey of certain of these forms of accommodation will reveal that the First Amendment commands not official hostility toward religion, but only a strict neutrality in matters of religion. . . .

It may be helpful for purposes of analysis to group these other practices and forms of accommodation into several rough categories.

A. *The Conflict Between Establishment and Free Exercise.*—There are certain practices, conceivably violative of the Establishment Clause, the striking down of which might seriously interfere with certain religious liberties also protected by the First Amendment. Provisions for churches and chaplains at military establishments for those in the armed services may afford one such example. The like provision by state and federal governments for chaplains in penal institutions may afford another example.

* * * * *

B. *Establishment and Exercises in Legislative Bodies.*—The saying of invocational prayers in legislative chambers, state or federal, and the appointment of legislative chaplains, might well represent no involvements of the kind prohibited by the Establishment Clause. Legislators, federal and state, are mature adults who may presumably absent themselves from such public and ceremonial exercises without incurring any penalty, direct or indirect. . . .

C. *Non-Devotional Use of the Bible in the Public Schools.*—The holding of the Court today plainly does not foreclose teaching *about* the Holy Scriptures or about the differences between religious sects in classes in literature or history. Indeed, whether or not the Bible is involved, it would be impossible to teach meaningfully many subjects in the social sciences or the humanities without some mention of religion. To what extent, and at what points in the curriculum, religious materials should be cited are matters which the courts ought to entrust very largely to the experienced officials who superintend our Nation's public schools.

* * * * *

D. *Uniform Tax Exemptions Incidentally Available to Religious Institutions.*— Nothing we hold today questions the propriety of certain tax deductions or exemptions which incidentally benefit churches and religious institutions, along with many secular charities and nonprofit organizations. If religious institutions benefit, it is in spite of rather than because of their religious character. For religious institutions simply share benefits which government makes generally available to education, charitable, and eleemosynary groups. There is no indication that taxing authorities have used such benefits in any way to subsidize worship or foster belief in God. And as among religious beneficiaries, the tax exemption or deduction can be truly nondiscriminatory, available on equal terms to small as well as large religious bodies, to popular and unpopular sects, and to those organizations which reject as well as those which accept a belief in God.

E. *Religious Considerations in Public Welfare Programs.*—Since government may not support or directly aid religious *activities* without violating the Establishment Clause, there might be some doubt whether nondiscriminatory programs of governmental aid may constitutionally include *individuals* who become eligible wholly or partially for religious reasons. For example, it might be suggested that where a State provides unemployment compensation generally to those who are unable to find suitable work, it may not extend such benefits to persons who are unemployed by reason of religious beliefs or practices without thereby establishing the religion to which those persons belong. Therefore, the argument runs, the State may avoid an establishment only by singling out and excluding such persons on the ground that religious beliefs or practices have made them potential beneficiaries. Such a construction would, it seems to me, require government to impose religious discriminations and disabilities, thereby jeopardizing the free exercise of religion, in order to avoid what is thought to constitute an establishment.

The inescapable flaw in the argument, I suggest, is its quite unrealistic view of the aims of the Establishment Clause. The Framers were not concerned with the effects of certain incidental aids to individual worshippers which come about as by-products of general and nondiscriminatory welfare programs . . . .

F. *Activities Which, Though Religious in Origin, Have Ceased to Have Religious Meaning.*—As we noted in our *Sunday Law* decisions, nearly every criminal law on the books can be traced to some religious principle or inspiration. But that does not make the present enforcement of the criminal law in any sense an establishment of religion, simply because it accords with widely held religious principles. . . .

This general principle might also serve to insulate the various patriotic exercises and activities used in the public schools and elsewhere which, whatever may have been their origins, no longer have a religious purpose or meaning. The reference to divinity in the revised pledge of allegiance, for example, may merely recognize the historical fact that our Nation was believed to have been founded "under God." Thus reciting the pledge may be no more of a religious exercise than the reading aloud of Lincoln's Gettysburg Address, which contains an allusion to the same historical fact.

* * * * *

WALZ v. TAX COMMISSION OF THE CITY OF NEW YORK

397 U. S. 664 (1970)

APPEAL FROM THE COURT OF APPEALS OF THE STATE OF NEW YORK

MR. JUSTICE BRENNAN, concurring.

I concur for reasons expressed in my opinion in *Abington School Dist.* v. *Schempp*, 374 U. S. 203, 230 (1963). I adhere to the view there stated that to give concrete meaning to the Establishment Clause,

> "the line we must draw between the permissible and the impermissible is one which accords with history and faithfully reflects the understanding of the Founding Fathers. It is a line which the Court has consistently sought to mark in its decisions expounding the religious guarantees of the First Amendment. What the Framers meant to foreclose, and what our decisions under the Establishment Clause have forbidden, are those involvements of religious

with secular institutions which (a) serve the essentially religious activities of religious institutions; (b) employ the organs of government for essentially religious purposes; or (c) use essentially religious means to serve governmental ends, where secular means would suffice. When the secular and religious institutions become involved in such a manner, there inhere in the relationship precisely those dangers—as much to church as to state—which the Framers feared would subvert religious liberty and the strength of a system of secular government. On the other hand, there may be myriad forms of involvements of government with religion which do not import such dangers and therefore should not, in my judgment, be deemed to violate the Establishment Clause." *Id.*, at 294–295.

Thus, in my view, the history, purpose, and operation of real property tax exemptions for religious organizations must be examined to determine whether the Establishment Clause is breached by such exemptions. See *id.*, at 293.

I

The existence from the beginning of the Nation's life of a practice, such as tax exemptions for religious organizations, is not conclusive of its constitutionality. But such practice is a facet of considerable import in the interpretation of abstract constitutional language. . . .

Rarely if ever has this Court considered the constitutionality of a practice for which the historical support is so overwhelming.

The Establishment Clause, along with the other provisions of the Bill of Rights, was ratified by the States in 1791. Religious tax exemptions were not an issue in the petitions calling for the Bill of Rights, in the pertinent congressional debates, or in the debates preceding ratification by the States. The absence of concern about the exemptions could not have resulted from failure to foresee the possibility of their existence, for they were widespread during colonial days. Rather, it seems clear that the exemptions were not among the evils that the Framers and Ratifiers of the Establishment Clause sought to avoid. Significantly, within a decade after ratification, at least four States passed statutes exempting the property of religious organizations from taxation.

Although the First Amendment may not have applied to the States during this period, practice in Virginia at the time is nonetheless instructive.

* * * * *

II

Government has two basic secular purposes for granting real propery tax exemptions to religious organizations. First, these organizations are exempted because they, among a range of other private, nonprofit organizations contribute to the well-being of the community in a variety of nonreligious ways, and thereby bear burdens that would otherwise either have to be met by general taxation, or be left undone, to the detriment of the community.

* * * * *

Second, government grants exemptions to religious organizations because they uniquely contribute to the pluralism of American society by their religious activities. . . .

III

Although governmental purposes for granting religious exemptions may be wholly secular, exemptions can nonetheless violate the Establishment Clause if they result in extensive state involvement with religion. Accordingly, those who urge the exemptions' unconstitutionality argue that exemptions are the equivalent of governmental subsidy of churches. General subsidies of religious activities would, of course, constitute impermissible state involvement with religion.

Tax exemptions and general subsidies, however, are qualitatively different. Though both provide economic assistance, they do so in fundamentally different ways. A subsidy involves the direct transfer of public monies to the subsidized enterprise and uses resources exacted from taxpayers as a whole. An exemption, on the other hand, involves no such transfer. It assists the exempted enterprise only passively, by relieving a privately funded venture of the burden of paying taxes. In other words, "[i]n the case of direct subsidy, the state forcibly diverts the income of both believers and nonbelievers to churches," while "[i]n the case of an exemption, the state merely refrains from diverting to its own uses income independently generated by the churches through voluntary contributions." Giannella, Religious Liberty, Nonestablishment, and Doctrinal Development, pt. II, 81 Harv. L. Rev. 513, 553 (1968). . . .

Even though exemptions produce only passive state involvement with religion, nonetheless some argue that their termination would be desirable as a means of reducing the level of church-state contact. But it cannot realistically be said that termination of religious tax exemptions would quantitatively lessen the extent of state involvement with religion. Appellee contends that "[a]s a practical matter, the public welfare activities and the sectarian activities of religious institutions are so intertwined that they cannot be separated for the purpose of determining eligibility for tax exemptions." If not impossible, the separation would certainly involve extensive state investigation into church operations and finances. Moreover, the termination of exemptions would give rise, as the Court says, to the necessity for "tax valuation of church property, tax liens, tax foreclosures, and the direct confrontations and conflicts that follow in the train of those legal processes." *Ante*, at 674. Taxation, further, would bear unequally on different churches, having its most disruptive effect on those with the least ability to meet the annual levies assessed against them. And taxation would surely influence the allocation of church resources. By diverting funds otherwise available for religious or public service purposes to the support of the Government, taxation would necessarily affect the extent of church support for the enterprises that they now promote. In many instances, the public service activities would bear the brunt of the reallocation, as churches looked first to maintain their places and programs of worship. In short, the cessation of exemptions would have a significant impact on religious organizations. Whether Government grants or withholds the exemptions, it is going to be involved with religion.

* * * * *

Chapter 7 LEWIS F. POWELL: THE THREE AND ONE-HALF PRONGED TEST

The notion that the Chief Justice of the Supreme Court of the United States is simply first among equals, primus inter pares, is one that is speedily dispelled in the first course in American Government. Whether he be one of the acknowledged greats such as a Hughes or a Warren, or one of the less notable, like a Vinson, to both the academic and layman, it is the Hughes or Warren or Vinson Court. Failure or success, "the Chief" indelibly puts his mark on the Court during his tenure as its leader.

Among the Associate Justices, also, all are not equal. Each may have only one vote in conference, but some clearly are more powerful than others. A Black or a Frankfurter, by dint of personality and/or perspicacity, played a role that far outdistanced a Minton or a Whittaker. Even less obviously outstanding jurists, given the right circumstances, can come to play a role quite disproportionate to their single vote.

Justice Tom Clark is one such case. President Harry Truman referred to the elevation of his Attorney General to the High Bench as "the biggest damn-fool mistake" he made as President. Regardless of Truman's opinion, Clark emerged as a key figure on the Warren Court in the late fifties and early sixties. His crucial fifth vote helped trigger the criminal rights revolution that today is seen as being so characteristic of the Warren era. An example from an earlier period is Justice Owen Roberts, whose crucial vote in *NLRB v. Jones and Loughlin Steel Corp.* (1937) produced "the switch in time that saved nine."

The fact is that during the sixteen years of the Burger Court neither a conservative nor a liberal bloc has had a solid majority. This situation may have changed in favor of the conservative bloc with the appointment by President Ronald Reagan of Sandra Day O'Connor to succeed Potter Stewart, and it will surely change if Reagan gets the opportunity to make further appointments during his second term. But this situation provides centrist Justices an excellent, indeed unparalleled, opportunity to exercise power out of proportion to their numbers. The additional fact that one member of this centrist group, Justice Lewis Powell, is also possibly the clearest legal thinker on the Court gives him an added advantage. (Byron White and Potter Stewart have been the other two most consistent members of the Court's center; Justice John Paul Stevens, although generally unpredictable early in his service on the Court seems to be gravitating to the Brennan-Marshall camp; Justice Harry Blackmun tends to ricochet, depending on the issue: liberal on abortion; conservative on criminal rights). A former president of the American Bar Association, Justice Powell appears very much "the lawyer's lawyer." If Hollywood casting directors would have picked Warren Burger as Chief Justice, they would surely have chosen Powell to play the role of senior partner in a prestigious law firm, albeit one based in Richmond!

Since Richard Nixon claimed that he wanted to appoint Justices who would follow in the footsteps of Felix Frankfurter, he chose well in Lewis Powell. Powell appears to be cut from much the same cloth as Frankfurter and Frankfurter's closest ally on the Court, Justice John Marshall Harlan. Like these two jurists, he tends to decide cases narrowly, perferring a "case by case" approach and eschewing sweeping ukases in the style of a Douglas or—at the other end of the ideological spectrum—a Rehnquist.

Powell's crucial role on the Burger Court has meant that he can be found in the majority on most cases and has also frequently given him the opportunity to write for the Court in some of the major decisions of recent years. *Regents of the University of California v. Bakke* (1978) is one such example. Four of the Justices would have upheld California-Davis Medical School's quota system for minority applicants as constitutional; four other Judges said that any use of race as a consideration for admission was a violation of Title VII of the Civil Rights Act. Powell found himself "in the catbird seat" and announced a Judgment of the Court that obviously reflected his views on the subject and on the matter of judicial decision making.

Perhaps a better example than *Bakke* of Powell's role within the Burger Court—better than *Bakke* because that decision, despite all the hoopla that surrounded it, has had little real effect except at California-Davis—is Powell's earlier decision in *San Antonio Independent School District v. Rodriguez* (1973). Here, Powell's interpretation of the equal protection clause effectively dashed the hopes of those who sought to expand the number of "suspect categories" and "fundamental rights" beyond those already established or explicitly found in the Constitution. Powell's opinion effectively reinterred the ghost of "substantive equal protection" that, according to the University of Texas's Wallace Mendelson, had reappeared toward the end of the Warren Court era. Powell has played a similarly important role in First Amendment cases, helping redefine "public figure" for purposes of libel (*Gertz v. Robert Welch, Inc.*–1974) and extending free speech guarantees to corporations (*First National Bank of Boston v. Bellotti*–1978). In the area of criminal rights, Powell's was the vote, in *Brewer v. Williams* (1977), that denied Chief Justice Burger an opportunity to overturn *Miranda v. Arizona* (1966)—a vote that earned him the icy scorn of "the Chief" for many weeks thereafter.

Powell's earlier decision in *Committee v. Nyquist* (1973) also could hardly have pleased Burger. *Nyquist* arose from efforts by New York's Governor Nelson Rockefeller to come up with a means by which the parents of children attending religious schools could be given some relief. Rockefeller had called upon the assistance of McGeorge Bundy, and the result was a statute that seemed to satisfy the demands of parochial school supporters and the demands of the First Amendment—at least as they had been interpreted by Chief Justice Burger in the cases of *Lemon v. Kurtzman* and *DiCenso v. Rhode Island* (1971). In these cases, Burger brought together for the first time the requirements of "secular purpose," "primary effect," and "no excessive entanglement." Regarding the Pennsylvania and Rhode Island statutes whereby religious school teachers who taught secular subjects had their salaries supplemented by state monies he found them to pass the first two tests, but to fail the third—because the state would be required "to provide for careful governmental controls and surveillance . . . in order to insure that state aid supports only secular education," thus "foster[ing] an impermissible degree of entanglement."

Given Burger's acceptance that the "primary effect" of the Pennsylvania and Rhode Island programs was not to aid religion, supporters of parochial aid were reasonably hopeful that the New York plan would be able to pass constitutional muster. The heart of the latter program was a system whereby parents would be reimbursed by the state for part of the costs of tuition. Since this aid went directly to the parents, the apparent danger of "excessive entanglement" seemed effectively skirted, and since the *Lemon* and *DiCenso* programs had vaulted by the "primary effect" hurdle, the New York plan appeared ready to clear the "wall of separation."

Justice Powell, however, disagreed. Speaking for a six-Justice majority, he struck the program down as unconstitutional, applying the *Lemon* test, to which the additional standard of "divisiveness" had now been fused. The resulting test remains, at least officially, the Court's basic tool in determining if legislation runs afoul of the requirements of the First Amendment. Whether the current Court—changed by the appointment of Sandra Day O'Connor (dubbed by one wag as "a Stanford twin" because of her ideological closeness to Justice Rehnquist, a fellow student at Stanford Law School) and no doubt influenced somewhat by the results of the Presidential elections of 1980 and 1984—will continue to adhere to this test is questionable (See Rehnquist: "A New Look at the Three-Pronged Test)." Whether "the three and one-half pronged" test is workable, in light of the Court's less than confidence-inspiring performance in *Wolman v. Walter* (1977)—or whether it is similar to the last efforts of the Warren Court to come up with a test of obscenity by taking all the various definitions of obscenity and hooking them together with bailing wire and a bevy of adverbs and adjectives—is another question that only time can answer.

COMMITTEE FOR PUBLIC EDUCATION & RELIGIOUS LIBERTY et al. *v.* NYQUIST, COMMISSIONER OF EDUCATION OF NEW YORK, et al.

APPEAL FROM THE UNITED STATES DISTRICT COURT FOR THE SOUTHERN DISTRICT OF NEW YORK

413 U. S. 756 (1973)

Mr. Justice Powell delivered the opinion of the Court.

James Madison, in his Memorial and Remonstrance Against Religious Assessments, admonished that a "prudent jealousy" for religious freedoms required that they never become "entangled . . . in precedents." His strongly held convictions, coupled with those of Thomas Jefferson and others among the Founders, are reflected in the first Clauses of the First Amendment of the Bill of Rights, which state that "Congress shall make no law respecting an establishment of religion, or prohibiting free exercise thereof." Yet, despite Madison's admonition and the "sweep of the absolute prohibitions" of the Clauses, this Nation's history has not been one of entirely sanitized separation between Church and State. It has never been thought either possible or desirable to enforce a regime of total separation, and as a consequence cases arising under these Clauses have presented some of the most perplexing questions to come before this Court. Those cases have occasioned thorough and thoughtful scholarship by several of this Court's most respected former Justices, including Justices Black, Frankfurter, Harlan, Jackson, Rutledge, and Chief Justice Warren.

As a result of these decisions and opinions, it may no longer be said that the Religion Clauses are free of "entangling" precedents. Neither, however, may it be said that Jefferson's metaphoric "wall of separation" between Church and State has become "as winding as the famous serpentine wall" he designed for the University of Virginia. *McCollum v. Board of Education*, 333 U. S. 203, 238 (1948) (Jackson, J., concurring). Indeed, the controlling constitutional standards have become firmly rooted and the broad contours of our inquiry are now well defined. Our task, therefore, is to assess New York's several forms of aid in the light of principles already delineated.

I

* * * * *

The first section of the challenged enactment, entitled "Health and Safety Grants for Nonpublic School Children," provides for direct money grants from the State to "qualifying" nonpublic schools to be used for the "maintenance and repair of . . . school facilities and equipment to ensure the health, welfare and safety of enrolled pupils."

* * * * *

The remainder of the challenged legislation—§§ 2 through 5—is a single package captioned the "Elementary and Secondary Education Opportunity Program." It is composed, essentially, of two parts, a tuition grant program and a tax benefit program. Section 2 establishes a limited plan providing tuition reimbursements to parents of children attending elementary or secondary nonpublic schools. To qualify under this section a parent must have an annual taxable income of less than $5,000. The amount of reimbursement is limited to $50 for each grade school child and $100 for each high school child. Each parent is required, however, to submit to the Commissioner of Education a verified statement containing a receipted tuition bill, and the amount of state reimbursement may not exceed 50% of that figure. No restrictions are imposed on the use of the funds by the reimbursed parents.

This section, like § 1, is prefaced by a series of legislative findings designed to explain the impetus for the State's action. Expressing a dedication to the "vitality of our pluralistic society," the findings state that a "healthy competitive and diverse alternative to public education is not only desirable but indeed vital to a state and nation that have continually reaffirmed the value of individual differences." The findings further emphasize that the right to select among alternative educational systems "is diminished or even denied to children of lower-income families, whose parents, of all groups, have the least options in determining where their children are to be educated." Turning to the public schools, the findings state that any "precipitous decline in the number of nonpublic school pupils would cause a massive increase in public school enrollment and costs," an increase that would "aggravate an already serious fiscal crisis in public education" and would "seriously jeopardize quality education for all children." Based on these premises, the statute asserts the State's right to relieve the financial burden of parents who send their children to nonpublic schools through this tuition reimbursement program. Repeating the declaration contained in § 1, the findings conclude that "[s]uch assistance is clearly secular, neutral and nonideological."

The remainder of the "Elementary and Secondary Education Opportunity Program," contained in §§ 3, 4, and 5 of the challenged law, is designed to provide a form of tax relief to those who fail to qualify for tuition reimbursement. Under these sections parents may subtract from their adjusted gross income for state income tax purposes a designated amount for each dependent for whom they have paid at least $50 in nonpublic school tuition. If the taxpayer's adjusted gross income is less than $9,000 he may subtract $1,000 for each of as many as three dependents. As the taxpayer's income rises, the amount he may subtract diminishes. Thus, if a taxpayer has adjusted gross income or $15,000, he may subtract only $400 per dependent, and if his income is $25,000 or more, no deduction is allowed. The amount of the deduction is not dependent upon how much the taxpayer actually paid for nonpublic school tuition, and is given in addition to any deductions to which the taxpayer may be entitled for other religious or charitable contributions. . . . Thus, comparable tax benefits pick up at approximately the point at which tuition reimbursement benefits leave off.

* * * * *

Although no record was developed in these cases, a number of pertinent generalizations may be made about the nonpublic schools which would benefit from these enactments. The District Court, relying on findings in a similar case recently decided by the same court, adopted a profile of these sectarian, nonpublic schools similar to the one suggested in the plaintiffs' complaint. Qualifying institutions, under all three segments of the enactment, could be ones that:

"(a) impose religious restrictions on admissions; (b) require attendance of pupils at religious activities; (c) require obedience by students to the doctrines and dogmas of a particular faith; (d) require pupils to attend instruction in the theology or doctrine of a particular faith; (e) are an integral part of the religious mission of the church sponsoring it; (f) have as a substantial purpose the inculcation of religious values; (g) impose religious restrictions on faculty appointments; and (h) impose religious restrictions on what or how the faculty may teach." 350 F. Supp. 655, 663.

Of course, the characteristics of individual schools may vary widely from that profile. Some 700,000 to 800,000 students, constituting almost 20% of the State's entire elementary and secondary school population, attend over 2,000 nonpublic schools, approximately 85% of which are church affiliated. And while "all or practically all" of the 280 schools entitled to receive "maintenance and repair" grants "are related to the Roman Catholic Church and teach Catholic religious doctrine to some degree." *id.*, at 661, institutions qualifying under the remainder of the statute include a substantial number of Jewish, Lutheran, Episcopal, Seventh Day Adventist, and other church affiliated schools.

Plaintiffs argued below that because of the substantially religious character of the intended beneficiaries, each of the State's three enactments offended the Establishment Clause.

* * * * *

II

The history of the Establishment Clause has been recounted frequently and need not be repeated here. . . .

It is enough to note that it is now firmly established that a law may be one "respecting an establishment of religion" even though its consequence is not to promote a "state religion," *Lemon* v. *Kurtzman*, 403 U. S. 602, 612 (1971), and even though it does not aid one religion more than another but merely benefits all religions alike. *Everson* v. *Board of Education, supra,* at 15. It is equally well established, however, that not every law that confers an "indirect," "remote," or "incidental" benefit upon religious institutions is, for that reason alone, constitutionally invalid. . . .

Most of the cases coming to this Court raising Establishment Clause questions have involved the relationship between religion and education. Among these religion-education precedents, two general categories of cases may be identified: those dealing with religious activities within the public schools, and those involving public aid in varying forms to sectarian educational institutions. While the New York legislation places this case in the latter category, its resolution requires consideration not only of the several aid-to-sectarian-education cases, but also of our other education precedents and of several important noneducation cases. For the now well-defined three-part test that has emerged from our decisions is a product of considerations derived from the full sweep of the Establishment Clause cases. . . .

As the recitation of legislative purposes appended to New York's law indicates, each measure is adequately supported by legitimate, nonsectarian state interests.

We do not question the propriety, and fully secular content, of New York's interest in preserving a healthy and safe educational environment for all of its school children. . . .

But the propriety of a legislature's purposes may not immunize from further scrutiny a law which either has a primary effect that advances religion, or which fosters excessive entanglements between Church and State. Accordingly, we must weigh each of the three aid provisions challenged here against these criteria of effect and entanglement.

A

The "maintenance and repair" provisions of § 1 authorize direct payments to nonpublic schools, virtually all of which are Roman Catholic schools in low-income areas. . . .

Absent appropriate restrictions on expenditures for these and similar purposes, it simply cannot be denied that this section has a primary effect that advances religion in that it subsidizes directly the religious activities of sectarian elementary and secondary schools.

* * * * *

B

New York's tuition reimbursement program also fails the "effect" test, for much the same reasons that govern its maintenance and repair grants. The state program is designed to allow direct, unrestricted grants of $50 to $100 per child (but no more than 50% of tuition actually paid) as reimbursement to parents in low-income brackets who send their children to nonpublic schools, the bulk of which is conceededly sectarian in orientation. To qualify, a parent must have earned less than $5,000 in taxable income and must present a receipted tuition bill from a nonpublic school.

There can be no question that these grants could not, consistently with the Establishment Clause, be given directly to sectarian schools, since they would suffer from the same deficiency that renders invalid the grants for maintenance and repair. . . . The controlling question here, then, is whether the fact that the grants are delivered to parents rather than schools is of such significance as to compel a contrary result.

* * * * *

The parent is not a mere conduit, we are told, but is absolutely free to spend the money he receives in any manner he wishes. There is no element of coercion attached to the reimbursement, and no assurance that the money will eventually end up in the hands of religious schools. The absence of any element of coercion, however, is irrelevant to questions arising under the Establishment Clause. In *School District of Abington Township* v. *Schempp, supra,* it was contended that Bible recitations in public schools did not violate the Establishment Clause because participation in such exercises was not coerced. The court rejected that argument, noting that while proof of coercion might provide a basis for a claim under the Free Exercise Clause, it was not a necessary element of any claim under the Establishment Clause. 374 U. S., at 222–223. MR. JUSTICE BRENNAN's concurring views reiterated the Court's conclusion:

> "Thus the short, and to me sufficient, answer is that the availability of excusal or exemption simply has no relevance to the establishment question, if it is once found that these practices are essentially religious exercises designed at least in part to achieve religious aims. . . ." *Id.*, at 288.

A similar inquiry governs here: if the grants are offered as an incentive to parents to send their children to sectarian schools by making unrestricted cash payments to them, the Establishment Clause is violated whether or not the actual dollars given eventually find their way into the sectarian institutions. Whether the grant is labeled a reimbursement, a reward, or a subsidy, its substantive impact is still the same.

*   *   *   *   *

Finally, the State argues that its program of tuition grants should survive scrutiny because it is designed to promote the free exercise of religion. The State notes that only "low-income parents" are aided by this law, and without state assistance their right to have their children educated in a religious environment "is diminished or even denied." . . . this Court repeatedly has recognized that tension inevitably exists between the Free Exercise and the Establishment Clauses, *e. g., Everson* v. *Board of Education, supra; Walz* v. *Tax Comm'n, supra,* and that it may often not be possible to promote the former without offending the latter. As a result of this tension, our cases require the State to maintain an attitude of "neutrality," neither "advancing" nor "inhibiting" religion. In its attempt to enhance the opportunities of the poor to choose between public and nonpublic education, the State has taken a step which can only be regarded as one "advancing" religion. However great our sympathy, *Everson* v. *Board of Education,* 330 U. S., at 18 (Jackson, J., dissenting), for the burdens experienced by those who must pay public school taxes at the same time that they support other schools because of the constraints of "conscience and discipline," *ibid.*, and notwithstanding the "high social importance" of the State's purposes, *Wisconsin* v. *Yoder*, 406 U. S. 205, 214 (1972), neither may justify an eroding of the limitations of the Establishment Clause now firmly emplanted.

C

Sections 3, 4, and 5 establish a system for providing income tax benefits to parents of children attending New York's nonpublic schools. In this Court, the parties have engaged in a considerable debate over what label best fits the New York law. Appellants insist that the law is, in effect, one establishing a system of tax "credits." The State and the intervenors reject that characterization and would label it, instead, a system of income tax "modifications." We see no reason to select one label over another, as the constitutionality of this hybrid benefit does not turn in any event on the label we accord it. As MR. CHIEF JUSTICE BURGER's opinion for the Court in *Lemon* v. *Kurtzman*, 403 U. S., at 614, notes, constitutional analysis is not a "legalistic minuet in which precise rules and forms must govern." Instead we must "examine the form of the relationship for the light that it casts on the substance."

* * * * *

In practical terms there would appear to be little difference, for purposes of determining whether such aid has the effect of advancing religion, between the tax benefit allowed here and the tuition grant allowed under § 2.

* * * * *

III

Because we have found that the challenged sections have the impermissible effect of advancing religion, we need not consider whether such aid would result in entanglement of the State with religion in the sense of "[a] comprehensive, discriminating, and continuing state surveillance." *Lemon* v. *Kurtzman*, 403 U. S., at 619. But the importance of the competing societal interests implicated here prompts us to make the further observation that, apart from any specific entanglement of the State in particular religious programs, assistance of the sort here involved carries grave potential for entanglement in the broader sense of continuing political strife over aid to religion.

* * * * *

One factor of recurring significance . . . is the potentially divisive political effect of an aid program. As MR. JUSTICE BLACK'S opinion in *Everson* v. *Board of Education, supra*, emphasizes, competition among religious sects for political and religious supremacy has occasioned considerable civil strife, "generated in large part" by competing efforts to gain or maintain the support of government. 330 U. S., at 8–9.

* * * * *

Our examination of New York's aid provisions, in light of all relevant considerations, compels the judgment that each, as written, has a "primary effect that advances religion" and offends the constitutional prohibition against laws "respecting an establishment of religion." We therefore affirm the three-judge court's holding as to §§ 1 and 2, and reverse as to §§ 3, 4, and 5.

It is so ordered.

Chapter 8 **WARREN E. BURGER: BALANCING FREE EXERCISE CLAIMS**

Braunfeld v. Brown (1961) and *Sherbert v. Verner* (1963) are separated by only two years, yet the two seem strangely at odds despite Justice Brennan's valiant effort to square his decision in *Sherbert* with Warren's opinion in *Braunfeld*. In fact, *Braunfeld* seems more closely related to the ideas espoused by Frankfurter in his *Barnette* dissent; i. e., free exercise does not exempt the citizen from compliance with general secular regulations such as the Sunday Closing Law, under which Braunfeld, an Orthodox Jew, had been prosecuted. *Sherbert* seems to head in a different direction by ordering the State of South Carolina to carve out an exception from its unemployment compensation laws for Sherbert because of her religious beliefs (Sherbert was a member of the Seventh-day Adventists).

Admittedly, Brennan does rely on Warren's test from *Braunfeld*: "if the purpose or effect of a law is to impede the observance of one or all religions or is to discriminate invidiously between religions, that law is constitutionally invalid even though the burden may be characterized as being only indirect." But Brennan makes a significant addition. According to Brennan, free exercise demands that "[w]e must . . . consider whether some compelling state interest . . . justifies the substantial infringement of [Sherbert's] First Amendment right." This requirement represents an almost 180 degree shift from Warren's position that "to strike down, without the most critical scrutiny, legislation which imposes only an indirect burden on the exercise of religion . . . would radically restrict the operating latitude of the legislatures." For Warren in *Braunfeld*, the burden is clearly upon the free exercise claimant; for Brennan in *Sherbert*, the burden is shifted to the state.

The advent of the Burger Court inevitably raised doubts as to the continued vitality of *Sherbert*. Burger, appointed by President Nixon, was expected to curb the excesses of the Warren Court. Obviously, this included the criminal rights decisions of the Warren Court, particularly *Mapp* (1961) and *Miranda* (1966). Just as clearly, it meant a less strict position in terms of what its advocates called "indirect aid" to religion. What it meant for free exercise was less clear. Did Nixon see free exercise as desirable or undesirable? Do Reagan and the New Right want an expansion or a contraction of individual rights under this clause of the Constitution?

Yoder gave the first answer as to how the Burger Court would proceed on this front. An Old Order Amish, Yoder refused to send his children, ages fourteen and fifteen, to school after they had completed the eighth grade, claiming this would cause them to violate "the Biblical injunction from the Epistle of Paul to the Romans, [to] 'be not conformed to this world. . . .'" The subsequent cases of *United States v. Lee* (1982) and *Bob Jones University v. United States* (1983) provided further opportunities for the Burger Court to develop a position on the free exercise clause. *Lee*, the lesser known of the two more recent cases, like *Yoder* involved the Amish. A self-employed farmer, Lee employed other Amish on his farm, but, for reasons of religion, refused to pay the employer's share of social security taxes. *Bob Jones University* presented a situation arising from a decision by the Internal Revenue Service to deny tax-exempt status to Bob Jones University because of the latter's refusal to admit ". . . applicants engaged in an interracial marriage or known to advocate interracial marriage or dating," a refusal grounded on the school authorities' reading of Scripture.

Burger assigned all three opinions to himself. The three, each quite different, gave the Chief Justice an excellent opportunity to put his mark on the Court's free exercise jurisprudence. Not surprisingly, Burger adopted for free exercise the same standard, an approach that involves balancing, that he has favored in issues dealing with freedom of the speech and of the press. The interests of the individual are to be balanced against the interests of the state. Universal school attendance for the Amish serves little purpose, given "the Amish qualities of reliability, self-reliance, and dedication to work . . . ." (*Yoder*); consequently, a free exercise claim on this score prevails. Payment of social security taxes (*Lee*) or rooting out segregation from American society (*Bob Jones*) are on a quite different plain. Here the government's needs dominate.

For Burger, the calculation is a necessary one: society's rules cannot be gutted by the "myriad exceptions flowing from a variety of beliefs." For the skeptic, it sounds all too reminiscent of Chief Justice Morrison Waite's cavalier treatment of religious minorities in *Reynolds* (1878): ". . . the professed doctrine of religious belief [cannot be made] superior to the law of the land . . . ," at least when there exists "an overriding governmental interest" (Burger in *Lee*) or where "governmental interest substantially outweighs whatever burden denial of tax benefits places on petitioners' exercise of their religious beliefs (Burger in *Bob Jones*)."

The excerpts that follow, from Burger's opinions in *Yoder*, *Lee*, and *Bob Jones*, give an excellent picture of the Court's current thrust.

WISCONSIN v. YODER ET AL.

CERTIORARI TO THE SUPREME COURT OF WISCONSIN

406 U. S. 205 (1972)

MR. CHIEF JUSTICE BURGER delivered the opinion of the Court.

*   *   *   *   *

Respondents Jonas Yoder and Wallace Miller are members of the Old Order Amish religion, and respondent Adin Yutzy is a member of the Conservative Amish Mennonite Church. They and their families are residents of Green County, Wisconsin. Wisconsin's compulsory school-attendance law required them to cause their children to attend public or private school until reaching age 16 but the respondents declined to send their children, ages 14 and 15, to public school after they completed the eighth grade. The children were not enrolled in any private school, or within any recognized exception to the compulsory-attendance law, and they are conceded to be subject to the Wisconsin statute.

On complaint of the school district administrator for the public schools, respondents were charged, tried, and convicted of violating the compulsory-attendance law in Green County Court and were fined the sum of $5 each. Respondents defended on the ground that the application of the compulsory-attendance law violated their rights under the First and Fourteenth Amendments. The trial testimony showed that respondents believed, in accordance with the tenets of Old Order Amish communities generally, that their children's attendance at high school, public or private, was contrary to the Amish religion and way of life. They believed that by sending their children to high school, they would not only expose themselves to the danger of the censure of the church community, but, as found by the county court, also endanger their own salvation and that of their children. The State stipulated that respondents' religious beliefs were sincere.

In support of their position, respondents presented as expert witnesses scholars on religion and education whose testimony is uncontradicted.

*   *   *   *   *

Although the trial court in its careful findings determined that the Wisconsin compulsory school-attendance law "does interfere with the freedom of the Defendants to act in accordance with their sincere religious belief" it also concluded that the requirement of high school attendance until age 16 was a "reasonable and constitutional" exercise of governmental power, and therefore denied the motion to dismiss the charges. The Wisconsin Circuit Court affirmed the convictions. The Wisconsin Supreme Court, however, sustained respondents' claim under the Free Exercise Clause of the First Amendment and reversed the convictions. A majority of the court was of the opinion that the State had failed to make an adequate showing that its interest in "establishing and maintaining an educational system overrides the defendants' right to the free exercise of their religion." 49 Wis. 2d 430, 447, 182 N. W. 2d 539, 547 (1971).

I

There is no doubt as to the power of a State, having a high responsibility for education of its citizens, to impose reasonable regulations for the control and duration of basic education. See, e. g., *Pierce* v. *Society of Sisters*, 268 U. S. 510, 534 (1925). Providing public schools ranks at the very apex of the function of a State. Yet even this paramount responsibility was, in *Pierce*, made to yield to the right of parents to provide an equivalent education in a privately operated system.

*   *   *   *   *

. . . [A] State's interest in universal education, however highly we rank it, is not totally free from a balancing process when it impinges on fundamental rights and interests, such as those specifically protected by the Free Exercise Clause of the First Amendment, and the traditional interest of parents with respect to the religious upbringing of their children so long as they, in the words of *Pierce*, "prepare [them] for additional obligations." 268 U. S., at 535.

It follows that in order for Wisconsin to compel school attendance beyond the eighth grade against a claim that such attendance interferes with the practice of a legitimate religious belief, it must appear either that the State does not deny the free exercise of religious belief by its requirement, or that there is a state interest of sufficient magnitude to override the interest claiming protection under the Free Exercise Clause. Long before there was general acknowledgment of the need for universal formal education, the Religion Clauses had specifically and firmly fixed the right to free exercise of religious beliefs, and buttressing this fundamental right was an equally firm, even if less explicit, prohibition against the establishment of any religion by government.

* * * * *

We come then to the quality of the claims of the respondents concerning the alleged encroachment of Wisconsin's compulsory school-attendance statute on their rights and the rights of their children to the free exercise of the religious beliefs they and their forebears have adhered to for almost three centuries. In evaluating those claims we must be careful to determine whether the Amish religious faith and their mode of life are, as they claim, inseparable and interdependent. A way of life, however virtuous and admirable, may not be interposed as a barrier to reasonable state regulation of education if it is based on purely secular considerations; to have the protection of the Religious Clauses, the claims must be rooted in religious belief. Although a determination of what is a "religious" belief or practice entitled to constitutional protection may present a most delicate question, the very concept of ordered liberty precludes allowing every person to make his own standards on matters of conduct in which society as a whole has important interests. Thus, if the Amish asserted their claims because of their subjective evaluation and rejection of the contemporary secular values accepted by the majority, much as Thoreau rejected the social values of his time and isolated himself at Walden Pond, their claims would not rest on a religious basis. Thoreau's choice was philosophical and personal rather than religious, and such belief does not rise to the demands of the Religion Clauses.

Giving no weight to such secular considerations, however, we see that the record in this case abundantly supports the claim that the traditional way of life of the Amish is not merely a matter of personal preference, but one of deep religious conviction, shared by an organized group, and intimately related to daily living. That the Old Order Amish daily life and religious practice stem from their faith is shown by the fact that it is in response to their literal interpretation of the Biblical injunction from the Epistle of Paul to the Romans, "be not conformed to this world. . . ." This command is fundamental to the Amish faith. Moreover, for the Old Order Amish, religion is not simply a matter of theocratic belief. As the expert witnesses explained, the Old Order Amish religion pervades and determines virtually their entire way of life, regulating it with the detail of the Talmudic diet through the strictly enforced rules of the church community.

* * * * *

The conclusion is inescapable that secondary schooling, by exposing Amish children to worldly influences in terms of attitudes, goals, and values contrary to beliefs, and by substantially interfering with the religious development of the Amish child and his integration into the way of life of the Amish faith community at the crucial adolescent stage of development, contravenes the basic religious tenets and practice of the Amish faith, both as to the parent and the child.

The impact of the compulsory-attendance law on respondents' practice of the Amish religion is not only severe, but inescapable, for the Wisconsin law affirmatively compels them, under threat of criminal sanction, to perform acts undeniably at odds with fundamental tenets of their religious beliefs. See *Braunfeld* v. *Brown*, 366 U. S. 599, 605 (1961). Nor is the impact of the compulsory-attendance law confined to grave interference with important Amish religious tenets from a subjective point of view. It carries with it precisely the kind of objective danger to the free exercise of religion that the First Amendment was designed to prevent. As the record shows, compulsory school attendance to age 16 for Amish children carries with it a very real threat of undermining the Amish community and religious practice as they exist today; they must either abandon belief and be assimilated into society at large, or be forced to migrate to some other and more tolerant region.

* * * * *

Wisconsin concedes that under the Religion Clauses religious beliefs are absolutely free from the State's control, but it argues that "actions," even though religiously grounded, are outside the protection of the First Amendment. But our decisions have rejected the idea that religiously grounded conduct is always outside the protection of the Free Exercise Clause. It is true that activities of individuals, even when religiously based, are often subject to regulation by the States in the exercise of their undoubted power to promote the health, safety, and general welfare, or the Federal Government in the exercise of its delegated powers. See, *e.g, Gillette* v. *United States*, 401 U. S. 437 (1971); *Braunfeld* v. *Brown*, 366 U. S. 599 (1961); *Prince* v. *Massachusetts*, 321 U. S. 158 (1944); *Reynolds* v. *United States*, 98 U. S. 145 (1879). But to agree that religiously grounded conduct must often be subject to the broad police power of the State is not to deny that there are areas of conduct protected by the Free Exercise Clause of the First Amendment and thus beyond the power of the State to control, even under regulations of general applicability. *E.g., Sherbert* v. *Verner*, 374 U. S. 398 (1963); *Murdock* v. *Pennsylvania*, 319 U. S. 105 (1943); *Cantwell* v. *Connecticut*, 310 U. S. 296, 303–304 (1940). This case, therefore, does not become easier because respondents were convicted for their "actions" in refusing to send their children to the public high school; in this context belief and action cannot be neatly confined in logic-tight compartments. *Cf. Lemon* v. *Kurtzman*, 403 U. S., at 612.

Nor can this case be disposed of on the grounds that Wisconsin's requirement for school attendance to age 16 applies uniformly to all citizens of the State and does not, on its face, discriminate against religions or a particular religion, or that it is

1. Agresto, John — SC & const. democracy
   84 → KF5130.A93

65) Keynes, Edward — SC v. Congress
   prayer, busing, abortion.
   JK1541.K49

97) Lee, Francis Graham — Ye
   BV741.L44

motivated by legitimate secular concerns. A regulation neutral on its face may, in its application, nonetheless offend the constitutional requirement for governmental neutrality if it unduly burdens the free exercise of religion. *Sherbert* v. *Verner, supra*; cf. *Walz* v. *Tax Commission*, 397 U. S. 664 (1970). The Court must not ignore the danger that an exception from a general obligation of citizenship on religious grounds may run afoul of the Establishment Clause, but that danger cannot be allowed to prevent any exception no matter how vital it may be to the protection of values promoted by the right of free exercise. By preserving doctrinal flexibility and recognizing the need for a sensible and realistic application of the Religion Clauses

> "we have been able to chart a course that preserved the autonomy and freedom of religious bodies while avoiding any semblance of established religion. This is a 'tight rope' and one we have successfully traversed." *Walz* v. *Tax Commission, supra,* at 672.

We turn, then, to the State's broader contention that its interest in its system of compulsory education is so compelling that even the established religious practices of the Amish must give way. Where fundamental claims of religious freedom are at stake, however, we cannot accept such a sweeping claim; despite its admitted validity in the generality of cases, we must searchingly examine the interests that the State seeks to promote by its requirement for compulsory education to age 16, and the impediment to those objectives that would flow from recognizing the claimed Amish exemption. See, *e. g., Sherbert* v. *Verner, supra; Martin* v. *City of Struthers*, 319 U. S. 141 (1943); *Schneider* v. *State*, 308 U. S. 147 (1939).

*   *   *   *   *

. . . [T]he evidence adduced by the Amish in this case is persuasively to the effect that an additional one or two years of formal high school for Amish children in place of their long-established program of informal vocational education would do little to serve those interests.

*   *   *   *   *

The State attacks respondents' position as one fostering "ignorance" from which the child must be protected by the State. No one can question the State's duty to protect children from ignorance but this argument does not square with the facts disclosed in the record. Whatever their idiosyncrasies as seen by the majority, this record strongly shows that the Amish community has been a highly successful social unit within our society even if apart from the conventional "mainstream." Its members are productive and very law-abiding members of society; they reject public welfare in any of its usual modern forms. The Congress itself recognized their self-sufficiency by authorizing exemption of such groups as the Amish from the obligation to pay social security taxes.

It is neither fair nor correct to suggest that the Amish are opposed to education beyond the eighth grade level. What this record shows is that they are opposed to conventional formal education of the type provided by a certified high school because it comes at the child's crucial adolescent period of religious development. Dr. Donald Erickson, for example, testified that their system of learning-by-doing was an "ideal system" of education in terms of preparing Amish children for life as adults in the Amish community, and that "I would be inclined to say they do a better job in this than most of the rest of us do." As he put it, "These people aren't purporting to be learned people, and it seems to me the self-sufficiency of the community is the best evidence I can point to—whatever is being done seems to function well."

* * * * *

The State, however, supports its interests in providing an additional one or two years of compulsory high school education to Amish children because of the possibility that some children will choose to leave the Amish community, and that if this occurs they will be ill-equipped for life. The State argues that if Amish children leave their church they should not be in the position of making their way in the world without the education available in the one or two additional years the State requires. However, on this record, that argument is highly speculative. There is no specific evidence of the loss of Amish adherents by attrition, nor is there any showing that upon leaving the Amish community Amish children, with their practical agricultural training and habits of industry and self-reliance, would become burdens on society because of educational shortcomings. Indeed, this argument of the State appears to rest primarily on the State's mistaken assumption, already noted, that the Amish do not provide any education for their children beyond the eighth grade, but allow them to grow in "ignorance." To the contrary, not only do the Amish accept the necessity for formal schooling through the eighth grade level, but continue to provide what has been characterized by the undisputed testimony of expert educators as an "ideal" vocational education for their children in the adolescent years.

There is nothing in this record to suggest that the Amish qualities of reliability, self-reliance, and dedication to work would fail to find ready markets in today's society. Absent some contrary evidence supporting the State's position, we are unwilling to assume that persons possessing such valuable vocational skills and habits are doomed to become burdens on society should they determine to leave the Amish faith, nor is there any basis in the record to warrant a finding that an additional one or two years of formal school education beyond the eighth grade would serve to eliminate any such problem that might exist.

* * * * *

For the reasons stated we hold, with the Supreme Court of Wisconsin, that the First and Fourteenth Amendments prevent the State from compelling respondents to cause their children to attend formal high school to age 16. Our disposition of this case, however, in no way alters our recognition of the obvious fact that courts are not school boards or legislatures, and are ill-equipped to determine the "necessity" of discrete aspects of a State's program of compulsory education. This should suggest that courts must move with great circumspection in performing the sensitive and delicate task of weighing a State's legitimate social concern when faced with religious claims for exemption from generally applicable educational requirements. It cannot be overemphasized that we are not dealing with a way of life and mode of education by a group claiming to have recently discovered some "progressive" or more enlightened process for rearing children for modern life.

Aided by a history of three centuries as an identifiable religious sect and a long history as a successful and self-sufficient segment of American society, the Amish in this case have convincingly demonstrated the sincerity of their religious beliefs, the interrelationship of belief with their mode of life, the vital role that belief and daily conduct play in the continued survival of Old Order Amish communities and their religious organization, and the hazards presented by the State's enforcement of a statute generally valid as to others. Beyond this, they have carried the even more difficult burden of demonstrating the adequacy of their alternative mode of continuing informal vocational education in terms of precisely those overall interests that the State advances in support of its program of compulsory high school education. In light of this convincing showing, one that probably few other religious groups or sects could make, and weighing the minimal difference between what the State would require and what the Amish already accept, it was incumbent on the State to show with more particularity how its admittedly strong interest in compulsory education would be adversely affected by granting an exemption to the Amish. *Sherbert* v. *Verner, supra.*

Nothing we hold is intended to undermine the general applicability of the State's compulsory school-attendance statutes or to limit the power of the State to promulgate reasonable standards that, while not impairing the free exercise of religion, provide for continuing agricultural vocational education under parental and church guidance by the Old Order Amish or others similarly situated. The States have had a long history of amicable and effective relationships with church-sponsored schools, and there is no basis for assuming that, in this related context, reasonable standards cannot be established concerning the content of the continuing vocational education of Amish children under parental guidance, provided always that state regulations are not inconsistent with what we have said in this opinion.

Affirmed.

UNITED STATES *v.* LEE

APPEAL FROM THE UNITED STATES DISTRICT COURT FOR THE
WESTERN DISTRICT OF PENNSYLVANIA

455 U. S. 252 (1982)

CHIEF JUSTICE BURGER delivered the opinion of the Court.

We noted probable jurisdiction to determine whether imposition of social security taxes is unconstitutional as applied to persons who object on religious grounds to receipt of public insurance benefits and to payment of taxes to support public insurance funds. 450 U. S. 993 (1981). The District Court concluded that the Free Exercise Clause prohibits forced payment of social security taxes when payment of taxes and receipt of benefits violate the taxpayer's religion. We reverse.

I

Appellee, a member of the Old Order Amish, is a farmer and carpenter. From 1970 to 1977, appellee employed several other Amish to work on his farm and in his carpentry shop. He failed to file the quarterly social security tax returns required for employers, withhold social security tax from his employees, or pay the employer's share of social security taxes.

In 1978, the Internal Revenue Service assessed appellee in excess of $27,000 for unpaid employment taxes; he paid $91—the amount owed for the first quarter of 1973—and then sued in the United States District Court for the Western District of Pennsylvania for a refund, claiming that imposition of the social security taxes violated his First Amendment free exercise rights and those of his Amish employees.

The District Court held the statutes requiring appellee to pay social security and unemployment insurance taxes unconstitutional as applied. 497 F. Supp. 180 (1980). The court noted that the Amish believe it sinful not to provide for their own elderly and needy and therefore are religiously opposed to the national social security system. The court also accepted appellee's contention that the Amish religion not only prohibits the acceptance of social security benefits, but also bars all contributions by Amish to the social security system. The District Court observed that in light of their beliefs, Congress has accommodated self-employed Amish and self-employed members of other religious groups with similar beliefs by providing exemptions from social security taxes. 26 U.S.C. § 1402(g). The court's holding was based on both the exemption statute for the self-employed and the First Amendment. . . .

* * * * *

The preliminary inquiry in determining the existence of a constitutionally required exemption is whether the payment of social security taxes and the receipt of benefits interferes with the free exercise rights of the Amish. The Amish believe that there is a religiously based obligation to provide for their fellow members the kind of assistance contemplated by the social security system. Although the Government does not challenge the sincerity of this belief, the Government does contend that payment of social security taxes will not threaten the integrity of the Amish religious belief or observance. It is not within "the judicial function and judicial competence," however, to determine whether appellee or the Government has the proper interpretation of the Amish faith; "[c]ourts are not arbiters of scriptural interpretation." *Thomas* v. *Review Bd. of Indiana Employment Security Div.*, 450 U. S. 707, 716 (1981). We therefore accept appellee's contention that both payment and receipt of social security benefits is forbidden by the Amish faith. Because the payment of the taxes or receipt of benefits violates Amish religious beliefs, compulsory participation in the social security system intereferes with their free exercise rights.

The conclusion that there is a conflict between the Amish faith and the obligations imposed by the social security system is only the beginning, however, and not the end of the inquiry. Not all burdens on religion are unconstitutional. See, *e. g.*, *Prince* v. *Massachusetts*, 321 U. S. 158 (1944); *Reynolds* v. *United States*, 98 U. S. 145 (1879). The state may justify a limitation on religious liberty by showing that it is essential to accomplish an overriding governmental interest. *Thomas, supra; Wisconsin* v. *Yoder*, 406 U. S. 205 (1972); *Gillette* v. *United States*, 401 U. S. 437 (1971); *Sherbert* v. *Verner*, 374 U. S. 398 (1963).

B

Because the social security system is nationwide, the governmental interest is apparent. The social security system in the United States serves the public interest by providing a comprehensive insurance system with a variety of benefits available to all participants, with costs shared by employers and employees. The social security system is by far the largest domestic governmental program in the United States today, distributing approximately $11 billion monthly to 36 million Americans. The design of the system requires support by mandatory contributions from covered employers and employees. This mandatory participation is indispensable to the fiscal vitality of the social security system. "[W]ide-spread individual voluntary coverage under social security . . . would undermine the soundness of the social security program." S. Rep. No. 404, 89th Cong., 1st Sess., pt. 1, p. 116 (1965). Moreover, a comprehensive national social security system providing for voluntary participation would be almost a contradiction in terms and difficult, if not impossible, to administer. Thus, the Government's interest in assuring mandatory and continuous participation in and contribution to the social security system is very high.

C

The remaining inquiry is whether accommodating the Amish belief will unduly interfere with fulfillment of the governmental interest. In *Braunfeld* v. *Brown*, 366 U. S. 599, 605 (1961), this Court noted that "to make accommodation between the religious action and an exercise of state authority is a particularly delicate task . . . because resolution in favor of the State results in the choice to the individual of either abandoning his religious principle or facing . . . prosecution." The difficulty in attempting to accommodate religious beliefs in the area of taxation is that "we are a cosmopolitan nation made up of people of almost every conceivable religious preference." *Braunfeld, supra,* at 606. The Court has long recognized that balance must be struck between the values of the comprehensive social security system, which rests on a complex of actuarial factors, and the consequences of allowing religiously based exemptions. To maintain an organized society that guarantees religious freedom to a great variety of faiths requires that some religious practices yield to the common good. Religious beliefs can be accommodated, see, *e.g., Thomas, supra; Sherbert, supra,* but there is a point at which accommodation would "radically restrict the operating latitude of the legislature." *Braunfeld, supra,* at 606.

Unlike the situation presented in *Wisconsin v. Yoder, supra,* it would be difficult to accommodate the comprehensive social security system with myriad exceptions flowing from a wide variety of religious beliefs. The obligation to pay the social security tax initially is not fundamentally different from the obligation to pay income taxes; the difference—in theory at least—is that the social security tax revenues are segregated for use only in furtherance of the statutory program. There is no principled way, however, for purposes of this case, to distinguish between general taxes and those imposed under the Social Security Act. If, for example, a religious adherent believes war is a sin, and if a certain percentage of the federal budget can be identified as devoted to war-related activities, such individuals would have a similarly valid claim to be exempt from paying that percentage of the income tax. The tax system could not function if denominations were allowed to challenge the tax system because tax payments were spent in a manner that violates their religious belief. See, *e. g., Lull* v. *Commissioner*, 602 F. 2d 1166 (CA4 1979), cert. denied, 444 U. S. 1014 (1980); *Autenrieth* v. *Cullen*, 418 F. 2d 586 (CA9 1969), cert. denied, 397 U. S. 1036 (1970). Because the broad public interest in maintaining a sound tax system is of such a high order, religious belief in conflict with the payment of taxes affords no basis for resisting the tax.

III

Congress has accommodated, to the extent compatible with a comprehensive national program, the practices of those who believe it a violation of their faith to participate in the social security system. In § 1402(g) Congress granted an exemption, on religious grounds, to self-employed Amish and others. Confining the § 1402(g) exemption to the self-employed provided for a narrow category which was readily identifiable. Self-employed persons in a religious community having its own "welfare" system are distinguishable from the generality of wage earners employed by others.

Congress and the courts have been sensitive to the needs flowing from the Free Exercise Clause, but every person cannot be shielded from all the burdens incident to exercising every aspect of the right to practice religious beliefs. When followers of a particular sect enter into commercial activity as a matter of choice, the limits they accept on their own conduct as a matter of conscience and faith are not to be superimposed on the statutory schemes which are binding on others in that activity. Granting an exemption from social security taxes to an employer operates to impose the employer's religious faith on the employees. Congress drew a line in § 1402(g), exempting the self-employed Amish but not all persons working for an Amish employer. The tax imposed on employers to support the social security system must be uniformly applicable to all, except as Congress provides explicitly otherwise.

Accordingly, the judgment of the District Court is reversed, and the case is remanded for proceedings consistent with this opinion.

Reversed and remanded.

BOB JONES UNIVERSITY v. UNITED STATES

CERTIORARI TO THE UNITED STATES COURT OF APPEALS FOR
THE FOURTH CIRCUIT

461 U. S. 574 (1983)

CHIEF JUSTICE BURGER delivered the opinion of the Court.

We granted certiorari to decide whether petitioners, nonprofit private schools that prescribe and enforce racially discriminatory admissions standards on the basis of religious doctrine, qualify as tax-exempt organizations under § 501(c) (3) of the Internal Revenue Code of 1954.

* * * * *

Based on the "national policy to discourage racial discrimination in education," the IRS ruled that "a [private] school not having a racially nondiscriminatory policy as to students is not 'charitable' within the common law concepts reflected in sections 170 and 501(c)(3) of the Code." *Id.*, at 231.

The application of the IRS construction of these provisions to petitioners, two private schools with racially discriminatory admissions policies, is now before us.

B

No. 81-3, Bob Jones University v. United States

Bob Jones University is a nonprofit corporation located in Greenville, S. C. Its purpose is "to conduct an institution of learning . . . , giving special emphasis to the Christian religion and the ethics revealed in the Holy Scriptures."

* * * * *

The sponsors of the University genuinely believe that the Bible forbids interracial dating and marriage. To effectuate these views, Negroes were completely excluded until 1971. From 1971 to May 1975, the University accepted no applications from unmarried Negroes, but did accept applications from Negroes married with their race.

Following the decision of the United States Court of Appeals for the Fourth Circuit in *McCrary* v. *Runyon*, 515 F. 2d 1082 (1975), aff'd, 427 U. S. 160 (1976), prohibiting racial exclusion from private schools, the University revised its policy. Since May 29, 1975, the University has permitted unmarried Negroes to enroll; but a disciplinary rule prohibits interracial dating and marriage. That rule reads:

"*There is to be no interracial dating.*
"1. Students who are partners in an interracial marriage will be expelled.
"2. Students who are members of or affiliated with any group or organization which holds as one of its goals or advocates interracial marriage will be expelled.
"3. Students who date outside of their own race will be expelled.
"4. Students who espouse, promote, or encourage others to violate the University's dating rules and regulations will be expelled." App. in No. 81-3, p. A197.

The University continues to deny admission to applicants engaged in an interracial marriage or known to advocate interracial marriage or dating. *Id.*, at A277.

Until 1970, the IRS extended tax-exempt status to Bob Jones University under § 501(c)(3). By the letter of November 30, 1970, that followed the injunction issued in *Green* v. *Kennedy*, 309 F. Supp. 1127 (DC 1970), the IRS formally notified the University of the change in IRS policy, and announced its intention to challenge the tax-exempt status of private schools practicing racial discrimination in their admissions policies.

*   *   *   *   *

Section 501(c)(3) . . . must be analyzed and construed within the framework of the Internal Revenue Code and against the background of the congressional purposes. Such an examination reveals unmistakable evidence that, underlying all relevant parts of the Code, is the intent that entitlement to tax exemption depends on meeting certain common-law standards of charity—namely, that an institution seeking tax-exempt status must serve a public purpose and not be contrary to established public policy.

This "charitable" concept appears explicitly in § 170 of the Code. That section contains a list of organizations virtually identical to that contained in § 501(c)(3). It is apparent that Congress intended that list to have the same meaning in both sections. In § 170, Congress used the list of organizations in defining the term "charitable contributions." On its face, therefore, § 170 reveals that Congress' intention was to provide tax benefits to organizations serving charitable purposes. The form of § 170 simply makes plain what common sense and history tell us: in enacting both § 170 and § 501(c)(3), Congress sought to provide tax benefits to charitable organizations, to encourage the development of private institutions that serve a useful public purpose or supplement or take the place of public institutions of the same kind.

Tax exemptions for certain institutions thought beneficial to the social order of the country as a whole, or to a particular community, are deeply rooted in our history, as in that of England. The origins of such exemptions lie in the special privileges that have long been extended to charitable trusts.

More than a century ago, this Court announced the caveat that is critical in this case:

"[I]t has now become an established principle of American law, that courts of chancery will sustain and protect . . . a gift . . . to public charitable uses, *provided the same is consistent with local laws and public policy. . . .* " *Perin* v. *Carey*, 24 How. 465, 501 (1861) (emphasis added).

Soon after that, in 1877, the Court commented:

"A charitable use, *where neither law nor public policy forbids,* may be applied to almost anything *that tends to promote the well-doing and well-being of social man.*" *Ould* v. *Washington Hospital for Foundlings*, 95 U. S. 303, 311 (emphasis added).

*   *   *   *   *

A corollary to the public benefit principle is the requirement, long recognized in the law of trusts, that the purpose of a charitable trust may not be illegal or violate established public policy. In 1861, this Court stated that a public charitable use must be "consistent with local laws and public policy," *Perin* v. *Carey*, 24 How., at 501. Modern commentators and courts have echoed that view. See, *e. g.*, Restatement (Second) of Trusts § 377, Comment *c* (1959); 4 Scott § 377, and cases cited therein; Bogert § 378, at 191–192.

When the Government grants exemptions or allows deductions all taxpayers are affected; the very fact of the exemption or deduction for the donor means that other taxpayers can be said to be indirect and vicarious "donors." Charitable exemptions are justified on the basis that the exempt entity confers a public benefit—a benefit which the society or the community may not itself choose or be able to provide, or which supplements and advances the work of public institutions already supported by tax revenues. History buttresses logic to make clear that, to warrant exemption under § 501(c)(3), an institution must fall within a category specified in that section and must demonstrably serve and be in harmony with the public interest. The institution's purpose must not be so at odds with the common community conscience as to undermine any public benefit that might otherwise be conferred.

B

We are bound to approach these questions with full awareness that determinations of public benefit and public policy are sensitive matters with serious implications for the institutions affected; a declaration that a given institution is not "charitable" should be made only where there can be no doubt that the activity involved is contrary to a fundamental public policy. But there can no longer be any doubt that racial discrimination in education violates deeply and widely accepted views of elementary justice.

*   *   *   *   *

Petitioners contend that, even if the Commissioner's policy is valid as to nonreligious private schools, that policy cannot constitutionally be applied to schools that engage in racial discrimination on the basis of sincerely held religious beliefs. As to such schools, it is argued that the IRS construction of § 170 and § 501(c)(3) violates their free exercise rights under the Religion Clauses of the First Amendment. This contention presents claims not heretofore considered by this Court in precisely this context.

This Court has long held the Free Exercise Clause of the First Amendment to be an absolute prohibition against governmental regulation of religious beliefs, *Wisconsin* v. *Yoder*, 406 U.S. 205, 219 (1972); *Sherbert* v. *Verner*, 374 U. S. 398, 402 (1963); *Cantwell* v. *Connecticut*, 310 U.S. 296, 303 (1940). As interpreted by this

Court, moreover, the Free Exercise Clause provides substantial protection for lawful conduct grounded in religious belief, see *Wisconsin* v. *Yoder, supra,* at 220; *Thomas* v. *Review Board of Indiana Employment Security Div.,* 450 U.S. 707 (1981); *Sherbert* v. *Verner, supra,* at 402–403. However, "[n]ot all burdens on religion are unconstitutional. . . . The state may justify a limitation on religious liberty by showing that it is essential to accomplish an overriding governmental interest." *United States* v. *Lee,* 455 U. S. 252, 257–258 (1982). See, *e.g., McDaniel* v. *Paty,* 435 U.S. 618, 628, and n. 8 (1978); *Wisconsin* v. *Yoder, supra,* at 215; *Gillette* v. *United States,* 401 U.S. 437 (1971).

On occasion this Court has found certain governmental interests so compelling as to allow even regulations prohibiting religiously based conduct. In *Prince* v. *Massachusetts,* 321 U. S. 158 (1944), for example, the Court held that neutrally cast child labor laws prohibiting sale of printed materials on public streets could be applied to prohibit children from dispensing religious literature. The Court found no constitutional infirmity in "excluding [Jehovah's Witness children] from doing there what no other children may do." *Id.,* at 171. See also *Reynolds* v. *United States,* 98 U. S. 145 (1879); *United States* v. *Lee, supra; Gillette* v. *United States, supra.* Denial of tax benefits will inevitably have a substantial impact on the operation of private religious schools, but will not prevent those schools from observing their religious tenets.

The governmental interest at stake here is compelling. As discussed in Part II—B, *supra,* the Government has a fundamental, overriding interest in eradicating racial discrimination in education—discrimination that prevailed, with official approval, for the first 165 years of this Nation's constitutional history. That governmental interest substantially outweighs whatever burden denial of tax benefits places on petitioners' exercise of their religious beliefs. The interests asserted by petitioners cannot be accommodated with that compelling governmental interest, see *United States* v. *Lee, supra,* at 259–260; and no "less restrictive means," see *Thomas* v. *Review Board of Indiana Employment Security Div., supra,* at 718, are available to achieve the governmental interest.

* * * * *

The judgments of the Court of Appeals are, accordingly.

Affirmed.

Chapter 9 WILLIAM H. REHNQUIST: A NEW LOOK AT THE THREE-PRONGED TEST

It was rather ironic that Justice William H. Rehnquist, a few weeks before the 1984 Presidential election, went out of his way to assure a law school audience that Presidents "have often only been partly successful" in shaping the Court. It was ironic because Rehnquist himself had proved to be the kind of Justice he was expected to become. The thesis that he expounded, however, has a strong basis in history, continuing even into recent years, when judicial appointments have received greater than normal scrutiny: the performances on the Court, for example, of Justices Blackmun, Powell, and Stevens would hardly seem to conform to what their Presidential sponsors, Presidents Nixon and Ford, were likely to expect.

William Hubbs Rehnquist has been different. Of the four Nixon appointees, he has proven to be easily the most predictable, almost consistently voting to uphold government's power to legislate, despite claims of individual rights' violations, and supporting greater autonomy for state decision making in the face of demands for a preemptive, federal role. Both positions seem very much in line with the spirit of self-restraint that Nixon sought in his appointees. Critics claim, however, that self-restraint requires the believer to slavishly follow previous decisions without deviation, even when such decisions are themselves a product of judicial activism. Such a misrepresentation of self-restraint seems conveniently designed to preserve holdings with which the critics agree; it ignores the fact that in the not-too-distant past it was jurists committed to self-restraint who went quietly about the business of reversing outright or sub silentio those earlier activist decisions that had effectively crippled the power of the federal government to regulate the economy. Appeals to a "double standard," to Justice Stone's famous footnote four in *U.S. v. Carolene Products* (1937)—which posited a stricter standard for judicial review of legislation touching on individual rights and liberties than that employed by courts when examining laws that affect property—also do not wash.

Rehnquist's tendency to vote along the lines his early proponents had hoped for and his detractors had feared is nowhere as clear as in the cases involving the establishment clause. Together with the Chief Justice, Rehnquist has championed a fairly broad—some would say loose—interpretation of what types of aid are permissible under the establishment clause. This stance must please those voters whose support of Presidents Nixon and Reagan presupposed that they would push programs that would aid religious schools and legislation that would return religion to public schools. Just as important, they might be expected to appoint to the Court individuals who would vote to sustain such legislation as constitutional.

Until 1983, Rehnquist and Burger had made little progress on this front; it could almost be said that they had failed completely: *Everson* (1947) and *Allen* (1968), both pre–Burger Court decisions, remained the only significant aid programs that had survived the Court's close scrutiny. The wall had withstood unexpectedly well the anticipated onslaught. This was never more clear than in the *Nyquist* (1973) case, crucial because it involved an aid program that had been more carefully crafted than previous packages to avoid the dangerous constitutional shoals upon which earlier programs had been broken. Here, to Burger and Rehnquist's great chagrin, their pro-aid position attracted only the support of Justice White, the author of the Court's *Allen* opinion—therefore scarcely a new convert to the cause of aid to religious schools.

The retirement of Justice Stewart in 1981 and his replacement by Reagan nominee Sandra Day O'Connor seems finally to have provided Rehnquist and Burger with the opportunity they needed to effect a change in establishment clause thinking. With O'Connor, they can finally count on a solid four-vote bloc, and increasingly they have won over Justice Powell—who appears to have shifted somewhat from the position he took in *Nyquist* and, despite the changes on the Court since his appointment in 1971, continues to be probably its most influential member.

This new majority has already had a profound impact, sometimes using the standard three-pronged test—from which any inquiry as to divisiveness seems to have been dropped—sometimes ignoring it, and certainly taking a generally more relaxed attitude, in its use, towards the concept of "primary effect." They have upheld the Nebraska legislature's appointment and payment of a chaplain (*Marsh v. Chambers*–1983) and the erection by the City of Pawtucket, Rhode Island, of a nativity scene (*Donnelly v. Lynch*–1984). Also (and definitely more important, despite the fact that it garnered much less publicity than the other two cases), they have sustained a Minnesota program giving parents who pay tuition or fees to religious schools the right to a state tax deduction for such expenses.

Whether this new majority has found the key to the establishment dilemma or not remains to be seen. Supporters of strict separation—disciples of Jefferson and Madison—will doubtless charge that the current Court's attitude, rather than satisfying proponents of aid, will simply embolden them to demand more. It may even retrigger claims for aid of the more "direct" type, such as in *Lemon*, and *DiCenso* (1971)—cases involving state supplements paid to the salaries of teachers of secular subjects in religious schools, held unconstitutional with only Justice White dissenting. Obviously, the Court's new attitude on establishment will also encourage those who have never accepted the controversial Warren Court opinion banning spoken prayers from public schools (*Abington Township v. Schempp*–1963). It gives even greater hope to those who push for "a moment of silence." The amicus brief, for instance, submitted by the office of the Delaware attorney general in the Alabama moment of silence case currently before the Court (1985) relies on the promise of Burger's opinion in *Lynch v. Donnelly* (1984) that "legislation will be held valid unless there is 'no question that the statute was motivated wholly by religious considerations.'" Proponents of the Moynihan-Packwood tax credit proposal also must be buoyed by the Rehnquist opinion in *Mueller v. Allen* (1983), though some of the more thoughtful of this group might wonder whether there is not a constitutional difference between tax credits such as they propose and the tax deductions upheld in the Minnesota case. Senator James Buckley (R–NY), an earlier Senate supporter of parochial school aid, urged the tax deduction route.

Two things seem clear: First, Rehnquist and Burger have much work to do in setting forth exactly what standards they are applying. Burger, in particular, in his repeated appeals to traditions " . . . deeply imbedded in the history . . . of this country" (*Marsh*) of " . . . an unbroken history of official acknowledgment by all three branches of government of the role of religion in American life . . . " (*Lynch*) rings a little hollow—sounding more like a Fourth of July speech than a Court opinion. It can hardly be maintained that everything done by Congress in the eighteenth century was constitutional, unless the Chief wishes to become an apologist for the Alien and Sedition Acts. Justice Brennan was right on target when he observed in his *Marsh* dissent that:

> Legislators, influenced by the passions and exigencies of the moment, the pressure of constituents and colleagues, and the press of business, do not always pass sober constitutional judgment on every piece of legislation they enact, and this must be assumed to be as true of the members of the First Congress as any other.

Second, however the Rehnquist–Burger approach to the establishment question evolves, it would seem to be a construct that has no consistent relation to developments in free exercise—even the free exercise opinions of Rehnquist and Burger. Any such effort to fashion decisions concerning one aspect of religious liberty that ignores developments in the other realm seems doomed to failure, however popular the immediate results of such decisions may be. In either the short or long run, the internal contradictions of such an approach will be seen, and having been spotted as political in intent, they will be rejected as nonjudicial by a public that largely still believes the Court should be nonpolitical.

If such contradictions are to be resolved, it is likely that the burden will fall on Rehnquist—a challenge that he will probably welcome.

The two opinions that follow—the facts are set forth in the opinions themselves—present an accurate picture of where the current Court's majority is with respect to establishment. The first, from *Mueller*, by Rehnquist; the second, from *Donnelly*, is by Burger.

VAN D. MUELLER and JUNE NOYES, PETITIONERS

v. CLYDE E. ALLEN, JR. et al

ON WRIT OF CERTIORARI TO THE UNITED STATES COURT OF APPEALS FOR THE EIGHTH CIRCUIT

U. S. (1983)

JUSTICE REHNQUIST delivered the opinion of the Court.

Minnesota allows taxpayers, in computing their state income tax, to deduct certain expenses incurred in providing for the education of their children. Minn. Stat. § 290.09(22). The United States Court of Appeals for the Eighth Circuit held that the Establishment Clause of the First and Fourteenth Amendments was not offended by this arrangement. Because this question was reserved in *Committee for Public Education* v. *Nyquist*, 413 U. S. 756 (1973), and because of a conflict between the decision of the Court of Appeals for the Eighth Circuit and that of the Court of Appeals for the First Circuit in *Rhode Island Federation of Teachers* v. *Norberg*, 630 F. 2d 855 (CA1 1980), we granted certiorari. ——— U. S. ——— (1982). We now affirm.

Minnesota, like every other state, provides its citizens with free elementary and secondary schooling. Minn. Stat. §§ 120.06, 120.72. It seems to be agreed that about 820,000 students attended this school system in the most recent school year. During the same year, approximately 91,000 elementary and secondary students attended some 500 privately supported schools located in Minnesota, and about 95% of these students attended schools considering themselves to be sectarian.

Minnesota, by a law originally enacted in 1955 and revised in 1976 and again in 1978, permits state taxpayers to claim a deduction from gross income for certain expenses incurred in educating their children. The deduction is limited to actual expenses incurred for the "tuition, textbooks and transportation" of dependents attending elementary and secondary schools. A deduction may not exceed $500 per dependent in grades K through six and $700 per dependent in grades seven through twelve. Minn. Stat. § 290.09.

Petitioners—certain Minnesota—taxpayers—sued in the United States District Court for the District of Minnesota claiming that § 290.09(22) violated the Establishment Clause by providing financial assistance to sectarian institutions. They named as respondents the Commissioner of the Department of Revenue of Minnesota and several parents who took advantage of the tax deduction for expenses incurred in sending their children to parochial schools. The District Court granted respondent's motion for summary judgment, holding that the statute was "neutral on its face and in its application and does not have a primary effect of either advancing or inhibiting religion." 514 F. Supp. 998, 1003 (D Minn. 1981). On appeal, the Court of Appeals affirmed, concluding that the Minnesota statute substantially benefited a "broad class of Minnesota citizens."

Today's case is no exception to our oft-repeated statement that the Establishment Clause presents especially difficult questions of interpretation and application. It is easy enough to quote the few words comprising that clause—"Congress shall make no law respecting an establishment of religion." It is not at all easy, however, [to] apply this Court's various decisions construing the Clause to governmental programs of financial assistance to sectarian schools and the parents of children attending those schools. Indeed, in many of these decisions "we have expressly or implicitly acknowledged that 'we can only dimly perceive the lines of demarcation in this extraordinarily sensitive area of constitutional law.'" *Lemon v. Kurtzman*, 403 U. S. 609, 612 (1971), quoted with approval in *Nyquist, supra*, at 761.

One fixed principle in this field is our consistent rejection of the argument that "any program which in some manner aids an institution with a religious affiliation" violates the Establishment Clause. *Hunt v. McNair*, 413 U. S. 734, 742 (1973). See, *e. g., Bradfield v. Roberts*, 175 U. S. 291 (1899); *Walz v. Tax Commission*, 397 U. S. 664 (1970). For example, it is now well-established that a state may reimburse parents for expenses incurred in transporting their children to school, *Everson v. Board of Education*, 330 U. S. 1 (1947), and that it may loan secular textbooks to all school-children within the state, *Board of Education v. Allen*, 392 U. S. 236 (1968).

Notwithstanding the repeated approval given programs such as those in *Allen* and *Everson*, our decisions also have struck down arrangements resembling, in many respects, these forms of assistance. See, *e. g., Lemon v. Kurtzman, supra; Levitt v. Committee for Public Education*, 413 U. S. 472 (1972); *Meek v. Pittenger*, 421 U. S. 349 (1975); *Wolman v. Walter*, 433 U. S. 229, 237–238 (1977). In this case we are asked to decide whether Minnesota's tax deduction bears greater resemblance to those types of assistance to parochial schools we have approved, or to those we have struck down. Petitioners place particular reliance on our decision in *Committee for Public Education* v. *Nyquist, supra,* where we held invalid a New York statute providing public funds for the maintenance and repair of the physical facilities of private schools and granting thinly disguised "tax benefits," actually amounting to tuition grants, to the parents of children attending private schools. As explained below, we conclude that § 290.09(22) bears less resemblance to the arrangement struck down in *Nyquist* than it does to assistance programs upheld in our prior decisions and those discussed with approval in *Nyquist.*

The general nature of our inquiry in this area has been guided, since the decision in *Lemon* v. *Kurtzman,* 403 U. S. 602 (1971), by the "three-part" test laid down in that case:

> "First, the statute must have a secular legislative purpose; second, its principle or primary effect must be one that neither advances nor inhibits religion . . . ; finally, the statute must not foster 'an excessive government entanglement with religion.'" *Id.,* at 612–613.

While this principle is well settled, our cases have also emphasized that it provides "no more than [a] helpful signpost" in dealing with Establishment Clause challenges. *Hunt* v. *McNair, supra,* 413 U. S., at 741. With this *caveat* in mind, we turn to the specific challenges raised against § 290.09(22) under the *Lemon* framework.

Little time need be spent on the question of whether the Minnesota tax deduction has a secular purpose. Under our prior decisions, governmental assistance programs have consistently survived this inquiry even when they have run afoul of other aspects of the *Lemon* framework. See, *e. g., Lemon* v. *Kurtzman, supra; Meek* v. *Pittenger, supra,* 421 U. S., at 363; *Wolman v. Walter, supra,* 433 U.S., at 236. This reflects at least in part, our reluctance to attribute unconstitutional motives to the states, particularly when a plausible secular purpose for the state's program may be discerned from the face of the statute.

* * * * *

We turn therefore to the more difficult but related question whether the Minnesota statute has "the primary effect of advancing the sectarian aims of the nonpublic schools." *Committee for Public Education* v. *Regan,* 444 U. S. 646, 662 (1980); *Lemon* v. *Kurtzman, supra,* 403 U. S., at 612–613. In concluding that it does not, we find several features of the Minnesota tax deduction particularly significant. First, an essential feature of Minnesota's arrangement is the fact that § 290.09(22) is only one among many deductions—such as those for medical expenses, Minn. Stat. § 290.09(10) and charitable contributions, Minn. Stat. § 290.21—available under the Minnesota tax laws. Our decisions consistently have recognized that traditionally "[l]egislatures have especially broad latitude in creating classifications and distinctions in tax statutes," *Regan* v. *Taxation with Representation* ——— U. S. ——— (1983), in part because the "familiarity with local conditions" enjoyed by legislators especially enables them to "achieve an equitable distribution of the tax burden." *Madden* v. *Kentucky*, 309 U. S. 83, 87 (1940). Under our prior decisions, the Minnesota legislature's judgment that a deduction for educational expenses fairly equalizes the tax burden of its citizens and encourages desirable expenditures for educational purposes is entitled to substantial deference.

Other characteristics of § 290.09(22) argue equally strongly for the provision's constitutionality. Most importantly, the deduction is available for educational expenses incurred by *all* parents, including those whose children attend public schools and those whose children attend non-sectarian private schools or sectarian private schools. Just as in *Widmar* v. *Vincent*, ——— U. S. ——— (1981), where we concluded that the state's provision of a forum neutrally "open to a broad class of nonreligious as well as religious speakers" does not "confer any imprimatur of State approval," so here: "the provision of benefits to so broad a spectrum of groups is an important index of secular effect."

In this respect, as well as others, this case is vitally different from the scheme struck down in *Nyquist*. There, public assistance amounting to tuition grants, was provided only to parents of children in *nonpublic* schools. This fact had considerable bearing on our decision striking down the New York statute at issue; we explicitly distinguished both *Allen* and *Everson* on the grounds that "In both cases the class of beneficiaries included *all* schoolchildren, those in public as well as those in private schools." 413 U. S., at 782, n. 38 (emphasis in original). Moreover, we intimated that "public assistance (*e. g.*, scholarships) made available generally without regard to the sectarian-nonsectarian or public-nonpublic nature of the institution benefited," *ibid.*, might not offend the Establishment Clause. We think the tax deduction adopted by Minnesota is more similar to this latter type of program than it is to the arrangement struck down in *Nyquist*. Unlike the assistance at issue in *Nyquist*, § 290.09(22) permits *all* parents—whether their children attend public school or private—to deduct their children's educational expenses. As *Widmar* and our other decisions indicate, a program, like § 290.09(22), that neutrally provides state assistance to a broad spectrum of citizens is not readily subject to challenge under the Establishment Clause.

* * * * *

Turning to the third part of the *Lemon* inquiry, we have no difficulty in concluding that the Minnesota statute does not "excessively entangle" the state in religion. The only plausible source of the "comprehensive, discriminating, and continuing state surveillance," 403 U. S., at 619, necessary to run afoul of this standard would lie in the fact that state officials must determine whether particular textbooks qualify for a deduction. In making this decision, state officials must disallow deductions taken from "instructional books and materials used in the teaching of religious tenets, doctrines or worship, the purpose of which is to inculcate such tenets, doctrines or worship." Minn. Stat. § 290.09(22). Making decisions such as this does not differ substantially from making the types of decisions approved in earlier opinions of this Court. In *Board of Education v. Allen*, 392 U.S. 236 (1968), for example, the Court upheld the loan of secular textbooks to parents or children attending nonpublic schools; though state officials were required to determine whether particular books were or were not secular, the system was held not to violate the Establishment Clause. See also *Wolman* v. *Walter, supra*; *Meek v. Pittenger, supra*. The same result follows in this case.

For the foregoing reasons, the judgment of the Court of Appeals is

Affirmed.

DENNIS LYNCH, ETC., ET AL., PETITIONERS *v.*
DANIEL DONNELLY ET AL.

ON WRIT OF CERTIORARI TO THE UNITED STATES COURT OF
APPEALS FOR THE FIRST CIRCUIT

U.S. (1984)

THE CHIEF JUSTICE delivered the opinion of the Court.

We granted certiorari to decide whether the Establishment Clause of the First Amendment prohibits a municipality from including a crèche, or Nativity scene, in its annual Christmas display.

I

Each year, in cooperation with the downtown retail merchants' association, the City of Pawtucket, Rhode Island, erects a Christmas display as part of its observance of the Christmas holiday season. The display is situated in a park owned by a nonprofit organization and located in the heart of a shopping district. The display is essentially like those to be found in hundreds of towns or cities across the Nation—often on public grounds—during the Christmas season. The Pawtucket display comprises many of the figures and decorations traditionally associated with Christmas, including, among other things, a Santa Claus house, reindeer pulling Santa's sleigh, candy-striped poles, a Christmas tree, carolers, cutout figures representing such characters as a clown, an elephant, and a teddy bear, hundreds of colored lights, a large banner that reads "SEASONS GREETINGS," and the crèche at issue. All components of this display are owned by the City.

The crèche, which has been included in the display for 40 or more years, consists of the traditional figures, including the Infant Jesus, Mary and Joseph, angels, shepherds, kings, and animals, all ranging in height from 5" to 5'. In 1973, when the present crèche was acquired, it cost the City $1365; it now is valued at $200. The erection and dismantling of the crèche costs the City about $20 per year; nominal expenses are incurred in lighting the crèche. No money has been expended on its maintenance for the past 10 years.

Respondents, Pawtucket residents and individual members of the Rhode Island affiliate of the American Civil Liberties Union, and the affiliate itself, brought this action in the United States District Court for Rhode Island, challenging the City's inclusion of the crèche in the annual display. The District Court held that the City's inclusion of the crèche in the display violates the Establishment Clause, *Donnelly* v. *Lynch*, 525 F. Supp. 1150, 1178 (D R. I. 1981), which is binding on the states through the Fourteenth Amendment. The District Court found that, by including the crèche in the Christmas display, the City has "tried to endorse and promulgate religious beliefs," 525 F. Supp., at 1173, and that "erection of the crèche has the real and substantial effect of affiliating the City with the Christian beliefs that the crèche represents." *Id.*, at 1177. This "appearance of official sponsorship," it believed, "confers more than a remote and incidental benefit on Christianity." *Id.*, at 1178. Last, although the court acknowledged the absence of administrative entanglement, it found that excessive entanglement has been fostered as a result of the political divisiveness of including the crèche in the celebration. *Id.*, at 1179–1180. The City was permanently enjoined from including the crèche in the display.

A divided panel of the Court of Appeals for the First Circuit affirmed. *Donnelly* v. *Lynch*, 691 F. 2d 1029 (1982). We granted certiorari, ——— U. S. ——— (1983), and we reverse.

* * * * *

This Court has explained that the purpose of the Establishment and Free Exercise Clauses of the First Amendment is

> "to prevent, as far as possible, the intrusion of either [the church or the state] into the precincts of the other." *Lemon* v. *Kurtzman*, 403 U. S. 602, 614 (1971).

At the same time, however, the Court has recognized that

> "total separation is not possible in an absolute sense. Some relationship between government and religious organizations is inevitable." *Ibid*.

In every Establishment Clause case, we must reconcile the inescapable tension between the objective of preventing unnecessary intrusion of either the church or the state upon the other, and the reality that, as the Court has so often noted, total separation of the two is not possible.

The Court has sometimes described the Religion Clauses as erecting a "wall" between church and state, see, *e. g., Everson* v. *Board of Education*, 330 U. S. 1, 18 (1947). The concept of a "wall" of separation is a useful figure of speech probably deriving from views of Thomas Jefferson. The metaphor has served as a reminder that the Establishment Clause forbids an established church or anything approaching it. But the metaphor itself is not a wholly accurate description of the practical aspects of the relationship that in fact exists between church and state.

* * * * *

The Court's interpretation of the Establishment Clause has comported with what history reveals was the contemporaneous understanding of its guarantees. A significant example of the contemporaneous understanding of the Clause is found in the events of the first week of the First Session of the First Congress in 1789. In the very week that Congress approved the Establishment Clause as part of the Bill of Rights for submission to the states, it enacted legislation providing for paid chaplains for the House and Senate. In *Marsh* v. *Chambers*, ——— U. S. ——— (1983), we noted that seventeen Members of that First Congress had been Delegates to the Constitutional Convention where freedom of speech, press and religion and antagonism toward an established church were subjects of frequent discussion. We saw no conflict with the Establishment Clause when Nebraska employed members of the clergy as official Legislative Chaplains to give opening prayers at sessions of the state legislature. *Id.*, at ———.

The interpretation of the Establishment Clause by Congress in 1789 takes on special significance in light of the Court's emphasis that the First Congress

> "was a Congress whose constitutional decisions have always been regarded, as they should be regarded, as of the greatest weight in the interpretation of that fundamental instrument," *Myers* v. *United States*, 272 U. S. 52, 174–175 (1926).

It is clear that neither the seventeen draftsmen of the Constitution who were Members of the First Congress, nor the Congress of 1789, saw any establishment problem in the employment of congressional Chaplains to offer daily prayers in the Congress, a practice that has continued for nearly two centuries. It would be difficult to identify a more striking example of the accommodation of religious belief intended by the Framers.

C

There is an unbroken history of official acknowledgment by all three branches of government of the role of religion in American life from at least 1789. Seldom in our opinions was this more affirmatively expressed than in Justice Douglas' opinion for the Court validating a program allowing release of public school students from classes to attend off-campus religious exercises. Rejecting a claim that the program violated the Establishment Clause, the Court asserted pointedly:

> "We are a religious people whose institutions presuppose a Supreme Being." *Zorach* v. *Clauson, supra,* at 313.

See also *Abington School District* v. *Schempp,* 374 U. S. 203, 213 (1963).

Our history is replete with official references to the value and invocation of Divine guidance in deliberations and pronouncements of the Founding Fathers and contemporary leaders. Beginning in the early colonial period long before Independence, a day of Thanksgiving was celebrated as a religious holiday to give thanks for the bounties of Nature as gifts from God. President Washington and his successors proclaimed Thanksgiving, with all its religious overtones, a day of national celebration and Congress made it a National Holiday more than a century ago. Ch. 167, 16 Stat. 168 (1870). The holiday has not lost its theme of expressing thanks for Divine aid any more than has Christmas lost its religious significance.

Executive Orders and other official announcements of Presidents and of the Congress have proclaimed both Christmas and Thanksgiving National Holidays in religious terms. And, by Acts of Congress, it has long been the practice that federal employees are released from duties on these National Holidays, while being paid from the same public revenues that provide the compensation of the Chaplains of the Senate and the House and the military services. See J. Res. 5, 23 Stat. 516 (1885). Thus, it is clear that Government has long recognized—indeed it has subsidized—holidays with religious significance.

Other examples of reference to our religious heritage are found in the statutorily prescribed national motto. "In God We Trust," 36 U. S. C. § 186, which Congress and the President mandated for our currency, see 31 U. S. C. § 324, and in the language "One nation under God," as part of the Pledge of Allegiance to the American flag. That pledge is recited by thousands of public school children—and adults—every year.

Art galleries supported by public revenues display religious paintings of the 15th and 16th centuries, predominantly inspired by one religious faith. The National Gallery in Washington, maintained with Government support, for example, has long exhibited masterpieces with religious messages, notably the Last Supper, and paintings depicting the Birth of Christ, the Crucifixion, and the Resurrection, among many others with explicit Christian themes and messages. The very chamber in which oral arguments on this case were heard is decorated with a notable and permanent—not seasonal—symbol of religion: Moses with Ten Commandments. Congress has long provided chapels in the Capitol for religious worship and meditation.

There are countless other illustrations of the Government's acknowledgment of our religious heritage and governmental sponsorship of graphic manifestations of that heritage. Congress has directed the President to proclaim a National Day of Prayer each year "on which [day] the people of the United States may turn to God in prayer and meditation at churches, in groups, and as individuals." 36 U. S. C. § 169h. Our Presidents have repeatedly issued such Proclamations. Presidential Proclamations and messages have also issued to commemorate Jewish Heritage Week, Proclamation No. 4844, 46 Fed. Reg. 25,077 (1981), and the Jewish High Holy Days, 17 Weekly Comp. Pres. Doc. 1058 (Sept. 29, 1981). One cannot look at even this brief resume without finding that our history is pervaded by expressions of religious beliefs such as are found in *Zorach, supra*. Equally pervasive is the evidence of accommodation of all faiths and all forms of religious expression, and hostility toward none. Through this accommodation, as Justice Douglas observed, governmental action has "follow[ed] the best of our traditions" and "respect[ed] the religious nature of our people." *Id.*, at 314.

III

This history may help explain why the Court consistently has declined to take a rigid, absolutist view of the Establishment Clause. We have refused "to construe the Religion Clauses with a literalness that would undermine the ultimate constitutional objective *as illuminated by history*," *Walz* v. *Tax Commission,* 397 U. S. 664, 671 (1970) (Emphasis added). In our modern, complex society, whose traditions and constitutional underpinnings rest on and encourage diversity and pluralism in all areas, an absolutist approach in applying the Establishment Clause is simplistic and has been uniformly rejected by the Court.

Rather than mechanically invalidating all governmental conduct or statutes that confer benefits or give special recognition to religion in general or to one faith—as an absolutist approach would dictate—the Court has scrutinized challenged legislation or official conduct to determine whether, in reality, it establishes a religion or religious faith, or tends to do so. See, *Walz, supra,* 669. Joseph Story wrote a century and a half ago:

> "The real object of the [First] Amendment was . . . to prevent any national ecclesiastical establishment, which should give to an hierarchy the exclusive patronage of the national government." 3 Story, Commentaries on the Constitution of the United States 728 (1833).

In each case, the inquiry calls for line drawing; no fixed, *per se* rule can be framed. The Establishment Clause like the Due Process Clauses is not a precise, detailed provision in a legal code capable of ready application. The purpose of the Establishment Clause "was to state an objective, not to write a statute." *Walz, supra,* at 668. The line between permissible relationships and those barred by the

Clause can no more be straight and unwavering than due process can be defined in a single stroke or phrase or test. The Clause erects a "blurred, indistinct, and variable barrier depending on all the circumstances of a particular relationship." *Lemon, supra,* at 614.

In the line-drawing process we have often found it useful to inquire whether the challenged law or conduct has a secular purpose, whether its principal or primary effect is to advance or inhibit religion, and whether it creates an excessive entanglement of government with religion. *Lemon, supra.* But, we have repeatedly emphasized our unwillingness to be confined to any single test or criterion in this sensitive area. See *e.g. Tilton* v. *Richardson,* 403 U. S. 672, 677–678 (1971); *Nyquist, supra,* 413 U. S., at 773. In two cases, the Court did not even apply the *Lemon* "test." We did not, for example, consider that analysis relevant in *Marsh, supra.* Nor did we find *Lemon* useful in *Larson* v. *Valente,* 456 U. S. 228 (1982), where there was substantial evidence of overt discrimination against a particular church.

* * * * *

The Court has invalidated legislation or governmental action on the ground that a secular purpose was lacking, but only when it was concluded there was no question that the statute or activity was motivated wholly by religious considerations.

* * * * *

The narrow question is whether there is a secular purpose for Pawtucket's display of the crèche. The display is sponsored by the City to celebrate the Holiday and to depict the origins of that Holiday. These are legitimate secular purposes. The District Court's inference, drawn from the religious nature of the crèche, that the City has no secular purpose was, on this record, clearly erroneous.

The District Court found that the primary effect of including the crèche is to confer a substantial and impermissible benefit on religion in general and on the Christian faith in particular. Comparisons of the relative benefits to religion of different forms of governmental support are elusive and difficult to make. But to conclude that the primary effect of including the crèche is to advance religion in violation of the Establishment Clause would require that we view it as more beneficial to and more an endorsement of religion, for example, than expenditure of large sums of public money for textbooks supplied throughout the country to students attending church-sponsored schools, *Board of Education* v. *Allen, supra,* expenditure of public funds for transportation of students to church-sponsored schools, *Everson* v. *Board of Education, supra;* federal grants for college buildings of church-sponsored institutions of higher education combining secular and religious education, *Tilton, supra;* noncategorical grants to church-sponsored colleges and universities, *Roemer* v. *Board of Public Works*, 426 U. S. 736 (1976); and the tax exemptions for church properties sanctioned in *Walz, supra*. It would also require that we view it as more of an endorsement of religion than the Sunday Closing Laws upheld in *McGowan* v. *Maryland*, 366 U. S. 420 (1961); the release time program for religious training in *Zorach, supra*; and the legislative prayers upheld in *Marsh, supra*.

We are unable to discern a greater aid to religion deriving from inclusion of the crèche than from these benefits and endorsements previously held not violative of the Establishment Clause. What was said about the legislative prayers in *Marsh, supra*, at ———, and implied about the Sunday Closing Laws in *McGowan* is true of the City's inclusion of the crèche: its "reason or effect merely happens to coincide or harmonize with the tenets of some . . . religions." See *McGowan, supra*, at 442.

* * * * *

The District Court found that there had been no administrative entanglement between religion and state resulting from the City's ownership and use of the crèche. 525 F. Supp., at 1179. But it went on to hold that some political divisiveness was engendered by this litigation. Coupled with its finding of an impermissible sectarian purpose and effect, this persuaded the court that there was "excessive entanglement." The Court of Appeals expressly declined to accept the District Court's finding that inclusion of the crèche has caused political divisiveness along religious lines, and noted that this Court has never held that political divisiveness alone was sufficient to invalidate government conduct.

Entanglement is a question of kind and degree. In this case, however, there is no reason to disturb the District Court's finding on the absence of administrative entanglement. There is no evidence of contact with church authorities concerning the content or design of the exhibit prior to or since Pawtucket's purchase of the crèche. No expenditures for maintenance of the crèche have been necessary; and since the City owns the crèche, now valued at $200, the tangible material it contributes is *de minimis*. In many respects the display requires far less ongoing day-to-day interaction between church and state than religious paintings in public galleries. There is nothing here, of course, like the "comprehensive, discriminating, and continuing state surveillance" or the "enduring entanglement" present in *Lemon, supra*, at 619–622.

The Court of Appeals correctly observed that this Court has not held that political divisiveness alone can serve to invalidate otherwise permissible conduct. And we decline to so hold today. This case does not involve a direct subsidy to church-sponsored schools or colleges, or other religious institutions, and hence no inquiry into potential political divisiveness is even called for, *Mueller* v. *Allen*, ——— U. S. ———, 103 S. Ct. 3062, 3071. n. 11 (1983). In any event, apart from this litigation there is no evidence of political friction or divisiveness over the crèche in the 40-year history of Pawtucket's Christmas celebration. The District Court stated that the inclusion of the crèche for the 40 years has been "marked by no apparent dissension" and that the display has had a "calm history." 525 F. Supp., at 1179. Curiously, it went on to hold that the political divisiveness engendered by this lawsuit was evidence of excessive entanglement. A litigant cannot, by the very act of commencing a lawsuit, however, create the appearance of divisiveness and then exploit it as evidence of entanglement.

We are satisfied that the City has a secular purpose for including the crèche, that the City has not impermissibly advanced religion, and that including the crèche does not create excessive entanglement between religion and government.

* * * * *

We hold that, notwithstanding the religious significance of the crèche, the City of Pawtucket has not violated the Establishment Clause of the First Amendment. Accordingly, the judgment of the Court of Appeals is reversed.

It is so ordered.

Chapter 10 CONCLUSION: BEYOND NEUTRALITY: TOWARD A TRUE NEUTRAL PRINCIPLE FOR THE RELIGION CAUSES

To criticize the Court is particularly easy with respect to its decisions involving church-state relations. The great sensitivity of the issues involved in these cases, the variety of contrasting views Americans have concerning religion, and the fluidity of these views in a society whose attitudes about religion seem to be constantly changing—these are factors which have complicated the Court's work in this realm immensely. It should be pointed out that unlike the Congress and the President, who have frequently sought to fish to their own advantage in these troubled waters, the Court must not only explain its actions but be quite aware that a decision in one case will have a direct effect on pending cases. Still, having said this, part of the problem in First Amendment cases arises from the Court's failure to present an overriding rationale for its decisions, too many of which merit Justice Owen Roberts's deprecating comparison to limited railroad tickets, good for one day and one way only.

Herbert Wechsler, Columbia University law professor, appeals for ''general, neutral principles'' in the realm of First Amendment jurisprudence. Certainly something approaching a neutral principle is desperately needed if the Court is to have any chance of persuading its various publics that its decisions are right and deserve to be respected.

The closest the Court has come to such a principle is the concept of neutrality first identified as being at the core of the First Amendment guarantees by Justice Black in *Everson*, when he noted, concerning the First Amendment, that "that Amendment requires the state to be a neutral in its relations with groups of religious believers and non-believers; but [it does] not require the state to be their adversary. State power is no more to be used so as to handicap religions than it is to favor them."

But what is neutrality? or as an Irishman once remarked: "Fine, we're to be neutral, but would you tell me whom are we to be neutral for?" For Justice Black, following in the tradition of Thomas Jefferson, neutrality was tilted in favor of the state. For Justice Stewart, perhaps more influenced by the thinking of Roger Williams, neutrality tended to favor religion.

For neither Justice, in fact for no Supreme Court jurist, has neutrality proved an effective, "general, neutral principle." In contrast, University of Chicago law professor Philip Kurland has fashioned out of the concept of neutrality the best current example of Wechsler's long-sought constitutional standard. According to Kurland, the religion clauses should be read as one, as stating a single precept:

> that government cannot utilize religion as a standard for action or inaction because these clauses, read together as they should be, prohibit classification in terms of religion either to confer a benefit or to impose a burden. . . .

The theoretical attractiveness of Kurland's position should not hide the fact that its acceptance would tend to gut the free exercise clause of its meaning, while simultaneously allowing major aid to schools associated with religious denominations. Nevertheless, the precept surely remains as attractive today as when first unveiled by Kurland in 1962. In fact, it is more alluring today, since the present Court majority, at least as evidenced by its most recent establishment clause rulings, *Mueller v. Allen* (1983), upholding tax deductions for tuition to religious schools; *Marsh v. Chambers* (1983), sustaining the payment of a chaplain for the Nebraska legislature; and *Lynch v. Donnelly* (1984), affirming a city-sponsored crèche display—seems unable to rationalize its decisions. The Court minority, possibly in reaction to the inadequate logic of the majority, has also taken some bizarre stands. Justice Brennan's apparent denial of all tax exemptions and deductions for religion, in *Mueller*, is a good example of the latter.

Simply put, the present Court majority appears to some to be reaching unprincipled decisions, which cast a shadow over the continuing validity of many of the Supreme Court's earlier rulings. For all practical purposes, the triad of decisions set out above indicates that the Court has pulled up from the anchorage of the three-pronged test and is now at sea without a compass. Accordingly, it can be expected in the near future to do the unexpected. In the process, it is splitting into two distinct blocs on establishment questions: a separationist bloc composed of Justices Brennan, Marshall, Stevens, and Blackman and an accommodationist grouping of the Chief Justice and Justices White, Rehnquist, and O'Connor—with Justice Powell, at least temporarily, holding the key vote. On free exercise issues, only Brennan and Marshall have demonstrated themselves to be firm supporters of religious minorities—but not so committed as to be sympathetic with the positions of Edwin Lee and Bob Jones University. In such a state, Kurland's approach would perhaps be an improvement, but at a cost that most of us, I daresay, would not be willing to accept.

A possible option for the Court is to reject neutrality as represented by either Kurland or the Court and try once again to ascertain the "intent of the framers," not being satisfied with mere reiterations of The Memorial and Remonstrance and the Virginia Bill for Establishing Religious Liberty. These documents are helpful, but they cannot direct us to the solution of the basic issue.

The purpose of the Bill of Rights, of which the First Amendment is a part, was to pinpoint those areas over which the federal government was powerless to legislate. The federalists, you will recall, had argued that such guarantees were unnecessary, that the federal government, as a government solely composed of delegated powers, accordingly had the right to legislate only in the areas specifically enumerated. The anti-Federalists, as history has shown, correctly rejected this argument. It would appear that the anti-Federalists better appreciated the nature of the document than Publius and the other authors of the Federalist Papers.

Government, according to the Bill of Rights, was to have no authority over religion. This idea is admittedly almost identical to the idea expressed by Madison in The Memorial and Remonstrance written in 1784 to oppose a proposal for the State of Virginia to provide aid to teachers of religion.

Argued Madison:

> 2. . . . [I]f religion be exempt from the authority of the society at large, still less can it be subject to that of the legislative body."

But how should we define *authority* here?

One approach to a definition is to go back to the debates, but not to pay attention solely to the activity of James Madison. In fact, a review of the proceedings reveals a name that has been largely passed over, the name of a representative from New Hampshire, Judge Samuel Livermore—the author of "Livermore's motion," and the man, according to such authorities as Canon Anson Phelps Stokes and Leo Pfeffer, who contributed "the main ideas and some of the wording of the First Amendment. . . ."

Livermore, as both a member of the New Hampshire state convention called to ratify the Constitution and a member of the First Congress, offered the following resolution: "Congress shall make no laws touching religion or to infringe the rights of Conscience." More significantly, he offered the resolution in place of a proposal of Madison that read "no national religion shall be established by law; nor shall the rights of conscience be infringed."

In speaking of Madison's motion, Livermore allowed that he " . . . was not satisfied with that amendment, but he did not wish them to dwell long on the subject. He thought it would be better if it was altered . . . " Whereupon, he introduced what is referred to as "Livermore's motion." Madison withdrew his, and Livermore's was adopted by a vote of "thirty-one for, and twenty against it." This was the final motion of the House on the subject, and since the House played the dominant role in the debates on religious liberty, Livermore's motion can be assumed to be as good a representation as Madison's of the feeling in that chamber on the subject.

It is to this idea, "no law touching religion," that I believe we should turn in order to ascertain the meaning of the religion clauses. However influential, Madison's Remonstrance and Jefferson's Bill for Establishing Religious Liberty were not voted on by the First Congress, nor is there any indication of support for the ideas of Roger Williams, despite Mark deWolfe Howe's proper championing of the Rhode Islander's major role in advancing the cause of religious liberty in America.

"No law touching religion" clearly indicates a desire to remove from the federal government any power or authority over religion—a restriction which the Fourteenth Amendment extends to the states—either through the due process clause, as argued by the majority of the Justices who have sat since 1937, or the privileges and immunities clause, as favored by Justice Black and John Hart Ely, Stanford law dean. It erects a wall of separation, yes, and not simply the Jeffersonian wall that seemed best designed to repel efforts by the church to dominate the state but one aimed at protecting the church from the state. Remember, the New Englanders wanted to protect their local Congregational churches from federal control.

The federal government (and, through the Fourteenth amendment, the states as well) lacks the authority to affect religion in any way. "No law respecting an establishment of religion" not only means no aid, but also no regulation. "No law touching religion" creates an environment in which religion is to succeed or fail on its own.

To accomplish this, religion and the state must be absolutely separate. The wall protects both church and state; its purpose is to ensure the least possible interference by the church in the activities of the state and of the state in the affairs of the church. "No law touching religion" means that government, to the greatest degree possible, should eschew any action that benefits religion or any laws that injure religion.

Laws providing aid to religious schools, whether in the form of books or buses, touch religion. Laws providing building loans to religiously-affiliated colleges or universities do likewise. Book loans have profoundly affected the type of education offered in Catholic schools, making it more and more similar to that offered at public schools. Catholic colleges anxious for federal aid have willingly shed much of their traditional character.

Laws regulating such institutions also "touch religion." Taxation surely represents "touching." If churches are to be excluded from benefits, as they should be, they should be excluded from certain duties as well. "The power to tax is the power to destroy."

Obviously, like many worshippers at the shrine of "neutral principles," I have found it easier to criticize the workmanship of the Court than to offer something in its place. The concept "no law touching religion" is not a "general, neutral principle" according to the standards of Herbert Wechsler. I do, however, offer the following as a starting point for such a principle—one that builds upon Mr. Justice William Brennan's sadly neglected standard put forth in *Schempp*:

> Neither can Government give, either directly or indirectly, any aid, money, services, or support to any religion or any religious organization nor can Government impose, directly or indirectly any burden, tax, or regulation on any religion, religious organization, or individual in the practice of his/her religion, unless such burden is required by a compelling state interest that can be achieved by no other means.

INDEX

Abington Township v. Schempp, 42, 48, 50, 52, 54, 57, 63, 64, 65, 68–69, 80, 102, 110
   Brennan concurrence, 58–68
   Stewart dissent, 43–47
Abraham, Henry, 19
accommodation of religion, 36, 117
   Brennan in *Abington Township v. Schempp*, 66–68
   Burger in *Lynch v. Donnelly*, 109–111
   Burger in *United States v. Lee*, 94, 95
   Douglas in *Zorach v. Clauson*, 37–40
   Harlan in *Sherbert v. Verner*, 25
   Stewart in *Abington Township v. Schempp*, 46–47
   Stewart in *Sherbert v. Verner*, 49
activism, 18–19, 101
Adamson v. California, 19
Alien and Sedition Acts, 102
Autenrieth v. Cullen, 94

Baker v. Carr, 52
balancing test, 5, 84–85
   Burger in *Wisconsin v. Yoder*, 86–87, 91–92
   Burger in *United States v. Lee*, 94
Ball, William, 3
Barron v. Baltimore, 28
Bill for Establishing Religious Freedom. *See* Virginia Bill for Establishing Religious Freedom
Bingham, John, 16
Black, Hugo, 5, 8, 19, 20, 21, 27–29, 36, 41, 51, 52, 53, 72, 75, 82, 116, 118
   opinion in *Everson v. Board*, 29–34
Blackmun, Harry, 49, 73, 100, 117
Blaine Amendment, 28, 62
"Bloudy Tenent," 8
Board of Education v. Allen, 5, 36, 101, 104, 106, 107, 112
Bob Jones University v. United States, 6, 84, 117
   Burger opinion, 95–99

Bradfield v. Roberts, 27, 104
Braunfield v. Brown, 4, 25, 47, 48, 49, 55, 56, 83–84, 88, 94
Brennan, William, 42, 51–54, 73, 80, 83, 102, 116, 117, 119
   concurring opinion in *Abington Township v. Schempp*, 58–68
   opinion in *Sherbert v. Verner*, 54–57
Brewer v. Williams, 74
Brown v. Board of Education, 7, 52
Buckley, James, 102
Bundy, McGeorge, 74
Burger, Warren, 4, 5, 6, 50, 52, 53, 73, 74, 81, 83–85, 101, 102, 103, 117
   opinion in *Bob Jones University v. United States*, 95–99
   opinion in *Lynch v. Donnelly*, 107–114
   opinion in *United States v. Lee*, 92–95
   opinion in *Wisconsin v. Yoder*, 85–92
Burton, Harold, 29

Cammarano v. United States, 25
Cantwell v. Connecticut, 44, 50, 52, 55, 88, 98
Cardozo, Benjamin, 8
child benefit
   in *Cochran v. Louisiana*, 36
Clark, Tom, 43, 51, 52, 72–73
Cochran v. Louisiana State Board of Education, 30, 36
coercion
   Brennan concurrence in *Abington Township v. Schempp*, 65–66
   Brennan concurrence in *Walz v. Tax Commission*, 70
   Douglas opinion in *Zorach v. Clauson*, 37, 38
   Powell opinion in *Committee v. Nyquist*, 80
   Stewart dissent in *Abington Township v. Schempp*, 42, 45–46
Committee for Public Education v. Regan, 105

122 / Wall of Controversy

Committee v. Nyquist, 5, 50, 74, 101, 103, 104, 105, 106, 112
  Powell opinion, 75–82
compelling state interest, 5, 52, 119
  Burger on, 89
Corwin, Edward, 62

Dennis v. United States, 35
DiCenso v. Rhode Island, 74, 102
divisiveness, 4, 5, 74, 101
  Burger in *Lynch v. Donnelly*, 113–114
  Powell in *Committee v. Nyquist*, 82
double standard, 101
Douglas, William O., 5, 19, 35–37, 51, 53, 73, 111
  opinion in *Zorach v. Clauson*, 37–40
Duncan v. Louisiana, 8

Eisenhower, Dwight D., 41, 42, 51
Ely, John Hart, 118
Engel v. Vitale, 44, 48, 58, 62
Epperson v. Arkansas, 50
equal protection clause, 57, 74
Erickson, Donald, 90
Everson v. Board of Education of Ewing Township, 4, 8, 19, 28, 36, 38, 44, 57, 78, 80, 82, 101, 104, 106, 109, 112, 116
  Black opinion, 29–34
"excessive entanglement," 4, 5, 74
  Brennan in *Walz v. Tax Commission*, 70–71
  Burger in *Lynch v. Donnelly*, 112–113
  Powell in *Committee v. Nyquist*, 79, 81
  Rehnquist in *Mueller v. Allen*, 106, 113
  Stewart in *Meek v. Pittenger*, 50

Farrington v. Tokushige, 23
First National Bank v. Bellotti, 74
flag salute ceremony, 19
Flast v. Cohen, 28
Follett v. McCormick, 55
Ford, Gerald, 100
Fortas, Abe, 51
Fourteenth Amendment, 17
  incorporation, 8, 17, 28, 32, 61–62, 118
Fowler v. Rhode Island, 45, 55
Frankfurter, Felix, 18–21, 29, 41, 52, 53, 72, 73, 75
  dissenting opinion in *West Virginia Board of Education v. Barnette*, 21–24
Freund, Paul, 62

Gertz v. Robert Welch, Inc., 74
Gianella, Donald, 70

Gillette v. United States, 88, 93, 99
Gitlow v. New York, 28
Goldberg, Arthur, 24
Green v. Kennedy, 95
Grosjean v. American Press Co., 55

Hamilton, Alexander, 3
Harlan, John Marshall, 73, 75
  concurrence in *Sherbert v. Verner*, 24, 26
Henry, Patrick, 9
Holmes, Jr., Oliver Wendell, 17, 18, 41
Howard, Jacob, 16
Howe, Mark deWolfe, 28, 118
Hughes, Charles Evans, 72
Hunt v. McNair, 53, 104, 105

incorporation, 8, 17, 19, 28, 32, 61–62, 118
Interstate Ry. v. Massachusetts, 33

Jackson, Robert, 19, 20, 29, 75, 76, 80
Jacobellis v. Ohio, 4
Jefferson, Thomas, 7, 8, 9, 22, 28, 31, 36, 59, 60, 62, 75, 76, 102, 109, 116, 118
  Bill for Establishing Religious Freedom, 9, 32, 117, 118

Kennedy, John F., 24
Kurland, Philip, 25, 42, 116, 117

Larson v. Valente, 112
Lemon v. Kurtzman, 4, 5, 50, 74, 78, 81, 88, 102, 104, 105, 106, 108, 112
Levitt v. Committee for Public Education, 104
Livermore, Samuel, 8, 16, 117–118
Lull v. Commissioner, 94
Lynch v. Donnelly, 102, 116
  Burger opinion, 107–114

McCollum v. Board, 36, 37, 38, 39–40, 44, 45, 76
McCrary v. Runyon, 96
McCulloch v. Maryland, 58
McDaniel v. Paty, 99
McGowan v. Maryland, 4, 44, 113
McKenna, Joseph, 51
McKinley, William, 51
Madden v. Kentucky, 106
Madison, James, 7, 8, 9, 14, 15–16, 22, 28, 31, 59, 60, 75, 102, 117, 118
  and First Amendment, 15–16
  and "Memorial and Remonstrance," 9–14, 31, 75, 118
Mapp v. Ohio, 84

Marsh v. Chambers, 102, 109, 112, 113, 116
Marshall, John, 28, 53, 73
Marshall, Thurgood, 42, 51, 117
Martin v. City of Struthers, 89
Meek v. Pittenger, 104, 105, 107
   Stewart judgment, 49–50
Memorial and Remonstrance, 9–14, 31–32, 75, 117
Mendelson, Wallace, 74
Minersville School District v. Gobitis, 19
Minton, Sherman, 72
Miranda v. Arizona, 74, 84
Morgan, Richard, 4
Monynihan-Packwood Tax Credit Bill, 102
Mueller v. Allen, 102, 113, 116
   Rehnquist opinion, 103–107
Murdock v. Pennsylvania, 28, 30, 50, 52, 55, 88
Murphy, Frank, 51
Murray v. Curlett, 42, 43, 48, 63
Myers v. United States, 109
Myrdal, Gunnar, 2

NAACP v. Button, 55
neutrality, 4, 29, 52, 104, 116
   Black in *Everson v. Board*, 34, 116
   Brennan in *Abington Township v. Schempp*, 61, 66
   Brennan in *Sherbert v. Verner*, 57
   Burger in *Wisconsin v. Yoder*, 88–89
   Clark in *Abington Township v. Schempp*, 43, 52
   Douglas in *Zorach v. Clauson*, 38–39
   Powell in *Committee v. Nyquist*, 80
   Rehnquist in *Mueller v. Allen*, 106
   Stewart in *Abington Township v. Schempp*, 46
New York Times Co. v. Sullivan, 52
Niemotko v. Maryland, 45
Nixon, Richard M., 18, 73, 84, 100, 101
NLRB v. Jones and Loughlin Steel Corporation, 73

Oaks, Dallin, 3, 4
O'Connor, Sandra Day, 42, 53, 73, 75, 101, 117
Ould v. Washington Hospital for Foundlings, 97
"overriding governmental interest," 85
   Burger in *United States v. Lee*, 93
   Burger in *Bob Jones University v. United States*, 99

Palko v. Connecticut, 8
Peckham, Horace, 27
Perin v. Carey, 97, 98
Pfeffer, Leo, 3, 117
Pierce v. Society of Sisters, 30, 34, 36, 44, 86
polygamy, 21
Powell, Lewis, 5, 29, 49, 72–75, 100, 101, 117
   opinion in *Committee v. Nyquist*, 75–82
Prince v. Massachusetts, 80, 88, 93, 99
"purpose and primary effect," 4, 5, 61, 74, 101
   Brennan in *Sherbert v. Verner*, 55
   Burger in *Lynch v. Donnelly*, 112
   Powell in *Committee v. Nyquist*, 79–80
   Rehnquist in *Mueller v. Allen*, 112–113

Reagan, Ronald, 73, 84, 101
Reed, Stanley, 20, 36
Regan v. Taxation with Representation, 106
Regents of the University of California v. Bakke, 73–74
Rehnquist, William, 42, 53, 73, 75, 100–103, 117
   opinion in *Mueller v. Allen*, 103–107
released time program, 37
Reynolds v. United States, 4, 21, 32, 33, 84, 88, 93, 99
Rhode Island Federation of Teachers v. Norberg, 103
Roberts, Owen, 20, 73, 115
Rockefeller, Nelson, 74
Roemer v. Board of Public Works, 113
Roth v. United States, 3, 52
Rutledge, Wiley, 19, 29, 75

San Antonio Independent School District v. Rodriguez, 74
Schneider v. State, 89
"secular purpose," 4, 5, 29, 74
   Burger in *Lynch v. Donnelly*, 112
   Powell in *Committee v. Nyquist*, 78–79
   Rehnquist in *Mueller v. Allen*, 105–112
secular regulation rule, 4
self-restraint, 19, 100–101
Sherbert v. Verner, 4, 5, 20, 42, 47, 52, 83–84, 88, 89, 91, 93, 98, 99
   Brennan opinion, 54–57
   Harlan dissent, 24–26
   Stewart concurrence, 48–49
"Ship Letter" of Roger Williams, 9
silent meditation, 42, 102
Spiro, Herbert, 2
Stevens, John Paul, 29, 42, 73, 100, 117

Stewart, Potter, 4–5, 41–43, 53, 73, 101, 116
  concurrence in *Sherbert v. Verner*, 48–49
  dissent in *Abington Township v. Schempp*, 43–47
  judgment in *Meek v. Pittenger*, 49–50
Stokes, Anson Phelps, 8, 117
Stone, Harlan Fiske, 20, 101
Story, Joseph, 111
"strict constructionist," 18

Thayer, James Bradley, 18
  on self-restraint, 19
Thomas v. Collins, 56
Thomas v. Review Board of Indiana Employment Security Division, 93, 94, 99
Thoreau, Henry, 87
three-pronged test, 4, 101–102, 116
  Powell opinion in *Committee v. Nyquist*, 75–82
  Rehnquist opinion in *Mueller v. Allen*, 105
  Stewart judgment in *Meek v. Pittenger*, 50
Tilton v. Richardson, 50, 112
Tocqueville, Alexis de, 1
Torcaso v. Watkins, 55, 56
Truman, Harry S., 51, 72
Tuttle, Charles H., 36

United States v. Butler, 21
United States v. Carolene Products, 101
United States v. Lee, 5–6, 84, 85, 99, 117

Burger opinion, 92–95
Uphaus v. Wyman, 52

Vinson, Fred, 72
Virginia Bill for Establishing Religious Liberty, 9, 32, 117, 118

Waite, Morrison, 21, 84
Walz v. Tax Commission, 4, 50, 53, 54, 80, 89, 104, 111, 113
  Brennan concurrence, 68–71
Warren, Earl, 5, 7, 41, 42, 51, 52, 72, 73, 75, 83–84, 102
Washington, George, 110
Wechsler, Herbert,
  on neutral principles, 115–116, 119
West Virginia State Board of Education v. Barnette, 19, 20, 59, 65
  Frankfurter dissent, 21–24
White, Byron, 5, 8, 24, 42, 53, 73, 117
Whittaker, Charles, 72
Widmar v. Vincent, 106
Williams, Roger, 7, 8–9, 28, 62, 116, 118
  "Ship Letter," 9
Wisconsin v. Yoder, 4, 5, 81, 84, 94, 98, 99
  Burger opinion, 85–92
Wolman v. Walter, 5, 29, 75, 104, 105, 107

Zorach v. Clauson, 19, 35, 36, 50, 58, 110, 113
  Douglas opinion, 37–40